Thank you
For Your Support

**Fox Run Environmental Education Center
is a 501c3 Non-Profit.
Our main focus:**

Environmental Education
Organic Gardening
Wildlife Conservation and Rehabilitation

Ame Vanorio, Founder

TABLE OF CONTENTS

TABLE OF CONTENTS 2

You can download this checklist for free from my website.

Medicine Cabinet Must Haves
Checklist For Squirrel Rescues

№	PRODUCTS	✓
1	Pedialyte	
2	Miracle Nipples - mini and original	
3	Heating Pad - no automatic shut-off	
4	Syringes - 1, 3, 5 ml for feeding; small needles for sub q fluids	
5	Gram Scale	
6	Chlorhexidine	
7	Bandages of various sizes	
8	Antibiotic First Aid Cream	
9	Disposable Gloves	
10	Tweezers, Q-Tips, and Scissors	
11	Pyrantel Pamoate wormer	
12	Saline Eye Solution	
13	Capstar - fleas and maggots	
14	Rodent/Squirrel Blocks	
15	Puppy Pads	
16	Towels - LOTS	
17	Meloxicam/Metacam (prescription)	
18	Baytril and/or Clavamox (prescription)	
19	Lactated Ringers/Saling Solutions (prescription)	

Introduction

Welcome to the wonderful world of wildlife rescue! If you love wildlife and want to help them this book is for you! You may be a wildlife rehabilitator, animal control officer, animal rescue volunteer, or someone who just loves wildlife and wants to help. This series is for you.

Squirrels live all over the world. This guide focuses on North American species and will discuss the care of infant and juvenile Grey, Red, Fox, and Flying Squirrels who are all tree squirrels. I also include information on Ground squirrels and Chipmunks.

This book takes a **deep dive specifically into rescuing squirrels**. What are the first steps when a squirrel has come into our care? What pests and diseases are they prone to and how to treat and prevent them? How should you feed an infant squirrel? How can I raise a squirrel so it is prepared to be released back into the wild? Why knowing their life cycle and natural history is so important.

If you want to know how to become a wildlife rehabilitator then check out my book **"Getting Started With Wildlife Rehabilitation"** also available on Amazon in paperback and Kindle.

This book is part of a wildlife rehabilitation series that consists of individual books that cover specific species. Each book has step-by-step instructions. Please note that some pests and diseases affect many species and will occur in several books, however, I focus on symptoms and treatments that are species-specific.

Legal Statement

Your state (or country) may have laws pertaining to rehabilitating squirrels and you should comply with those laws for the best care of the animals.

Each state has its own guidelines for becoming a wildlife rehabilitator and providing care for infant wildlife. These are typically listed under the state's Department of Fish and Wildlife or the Department of Natural Resources.

My wildlife rehabilitation and conservation career and experience have taken place in the USA. If you are in another country what's a common disease or animal for me may not be as common for you and vice versa.

My books are meant to help you recognize and treat common problems that present themselves with animals in your care. It should in no way replace advice given by your veterinarian. I assume that you are working with your veterinarian to provide the best possible outcomes.

I also recommend that new wildlife rehabilitators spend some time working with an experienced rehabber to "learn the ropes".

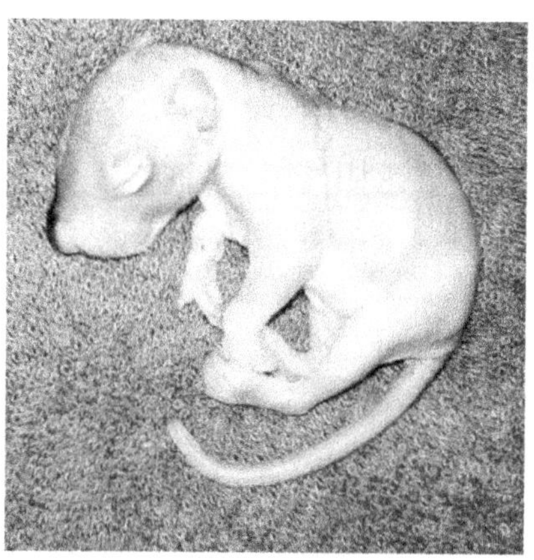

4 - 5 day old Eastern Grey Squirrel Photo by Ame Vanorio

Why?

I often get asked why I rehabilitate squirrels (besides the fact that they are cute). After all, squirrels are rodents and in plentiful supply.

Squirrel rehabilitation not only helps individual animals but also supports the broader ecosystem. By rehabilitating squirrels, we contribute to the well-being of habitats, enhance our local biodiversity, and help trees grow.

We promote a compassionate approach to interacting with wildlife. We teach our fellow humans the importance of wildlife in our backyards and beyond and humane ways to deal with conflicts.

Many times our rehab animals come to us through human error. Trees with baby squirrels are cut down or parents are trapped and killed for getting into houses. Domestic cats hunt squirrels.

Helping squirrels is a way to make that right. It's an act of compassion from one species to another.

Squirrels bring me joy. They are fun, courageous, fascinating, and make me laugh. I just want to return the favor.

Need some talking points on why we need to rescue squirrels?

Squirrels play a crucial role in maintaining the balance of ecosystems. They provide seed dispersal, which helps in planting new trees and forest diversity. In addition, their hidden caches are discovered by other animals, providing food for a variety of species.

The University of Wisconsin College of Veterinary Medicine states in their article *Celebrating Squirrels, the Ecosystem's Greatest Gardeners* "Squirrels are natural gardeners in oak savannas and prairies. In Southern Wisconsin, their stewardship is especially important because various native types of grassland are endangered".

Squirrels are a vital part of the food web. They are quite frankly, an important prey food. Many animals depend on squirrels for food. By rescuing them we participate in the circle of life. They serve as prey for various predators, including birds of prey, foxes, and snakes. Their presence supports the health and balance of populations.

Rehabilitation prevents unnecessary suffering and gives injured or orphaned squirrels a second chance at life. It is an act of compassion and empathy towards other beings.

Educating the public about squirrel behavior and needs can reduce human-wildlife conflicts. Understanding squirrels can lead to more harmonious coexistence in urban and suburban areas.

Common Reasons for Squirrel Intervention

Vehicle Collisions:
Squirrels get hit by cars while crossing roads. Depending on food sources the Eastern Gray Squirrel range is 1 - 7 acres which often has them crossing roads.

Predator Attacks:
Injuries from attacks by domestic pets (cats and dogs), birds of prey, or other wild predators. Cat bites especially need medical intervention.

Falls:
Falling from trees or power lines leads to fractures or other injuries. Falls that happen during tree work are a major cause of baby squirrel injuries.

Orphaned or Abandoned
The mother may have been killed by a predator, vehicle, or other incidents, leaving babies orphaned. Tree work may frighten her away.

Nest Disturbance:
Storms, tree cutting, or other human activities can destroy nests, causing babies to be separated from their mothers.

Disease
Mange: Caused by mites, leading to hair loss and skin infections.
Viral or Bacterial Infections: Such as squirrel pox, can cause severe health issues and require intervention.

Poisoning
Pesticides and Rodenticides: Accidental ingestion of chemicals used in gardens or around homes. Including pesticides and traps used for mice.

How To Tell If A Baby Squirrel Needs Intervention?

If you find a wild baby, look around to see if you see mom. She might be running around anxiously or chittering at you. We never want to create an orphan. A wild mom is the best possible mother for the baby.

If you see baby mammals on the side of the road look around and see if you see mom's body. A dead mom tells you these babies are orphans and need intervention.

Call your local rehabilitator or veterinarian for advice if you are unsure what to do.

Signs that babies may be orphans are:

- Dehydration over 5% or emaciation
- Covered in parasites such as fleas, ticks, and/or lice
- Matted or dirty fur
- Crying and moving in a circular manner
- Wounds with bleeding, exposed organs, or maggots.
- Possible concussion. Has been hit by car or fallen from tree
- Breathing problems
- In shock or unconscious
- Cold, low body temperature

Reuniting

Spring storms may knock nests out of trees. Sometimes there is a chance to reunite the family. If the baby is uninjured and the mom is nearby place the baby in a box or basket with a soft towel and hang it from a tree.

The box should be shallow because a large box may frighten Mom from entering. If the weather is chilly put in a "hot hands" hand warmer wrapped in a small towel or washcloth in a corner of the box.

If the baby is mobile place the box at the bottom of the tree in case they climb out. Observe from a distance to see if mom comes and gets the baby. This way you can also monitor any neighborhood cats that are allowed outside.

Reuniting chipmunks and ground squirrels can be a little bit different. They both nest in deep burrows which can be disturbed during excavation work. Sometimes the nests are dug out by dogs.
If the den is not destroyed and the babies appear ok you can try to put the den back together. Observe the area for 12 hours to see if mom comes back.

Make A Wildlife Rescue Car Kit

- Safety vest
- Flashlight
- Leather gloves
- Goggles
- Cat carrier
- Towels
- Piece of cardboard
- Hand warmers
- Wire cutters

Place everything in the cat carrier or a sturdy box and tuck into the back of your car

Important Numbers
Print out a list of your states licensed wildlife rehabilitators

Be Safe! Always make sure that you pull over in a safe spot and consider traffic when checking on the animal. Put on your emergency blinkers.

Don't let children handle or play with the baby. This is NOT the time for a selfie!

You can watch my video on making a wildlife rescue car kit. @foxruneec

Squirrel Fun Facts

- Their thick bushy tails provide balance and temperature regulation.
- They have excellent vision and a good sense of touch.
- They live an average of five to ten years in the wild and up to twenty in captivity.
- They have long front teeth incisors that grow continuously.
- A group of squirrels is called a "dray" or a "scurry".

Squirrels have unique hind ankles. Back ankles can rotate 180 degrees. this allows them to climb done a tree headfirst and dig there claws in so they don't pitch forward. No wonder they are so agile!

Squirrels will "sploot" in hot weather. They will lay belly down on a cool surface to bring their temperature down.

First Steps:
- Heat
- Hydration
- Formula Feeding

I will get into more species specific information below. But this advice applies to any squirrel or chipmunk baby that comes into your care.
ALL incoming baby squirrels need heat, hydration, and then after at least 12 hours, food.

Heat

The first step is to gradually warm the baby squirrel. Infant squirrels are most likely chilled because they depend on a mom to keep them warm. An older baby with open eyes is capable of thermoregulating however due to shock and/or trauma their body may not be providing necessary heat.

Depending on the squirrel species their normal body temperature is between 97–100°F (37°C) year-round. Gray squirrels can have a normal body temperature of 99–101°F (37.4–38.5°C), while fox squirrels is slightly higher.

Caution is needed when giving supplemental heat. A neonate or other animal that can't move should never be placed directly on the heat source. They may become overheated and unable to escape.

Siblings can be kept together and they will snuggle and help keep each other warm.

You can place newspapers or towels over the heating pad. I typically place the infant in a knitted pouch and place them just off the heating pad. Then I keep a thermometer in the carrier or cage to monitor the air temperature.

For a baby who is mobile, place a heating pad on low under one-half of the carrier. Then the baby has the option of crawling on or off the heated area.

The heating pad is the most commonly used way to offer heat. They are relatively inexpensive and easy to find. When you purchase a heating pad make sure you get on without an automatic shut-off. More and more have these as a safety method but it makes it very inconvenient for those of us who need to warm wildlife 24/7.

I like the Marunda brand just because it's made for pets and has a couple of nice features such as chew-resistant cords and a wipe-off surface. Squirrels, even small ones, like to chew so make sure you are checking on any heating pad that is inside the enclosure.

As your babies grow you can place the heating pad under the enclosure so they can not chew on it.

Heating pads also need to be monitored to make sure they are putting out consistent heat. You will also need to make sure the baby is not too hot or too cold.

If you have an incubator Carol Hardee (see Resources) recommends a temperature setting of "90-95 degrees Fahrenheit for squirrels without fur or those just beginning to grow fur and 85-90 degrees Fahrenheit for fully furred babies".

Always use common sense. Place your own hand in the enclosure and make sure the baby is warm but not too hot!

Rehydration

Dehydration can kill a baby much faster than lack of food. Baby animals should never be offered food until after they are rehydrated. Food, and formula is food, can actually cause their system to shut down.

Even an animal that seems perfectly hydrated should receive fluids to help them transition to new foods. I give everything fluids to start with. Rehydrate babies for 12 hours and for at least 4 feedings.

The process of rehydration begins after warming the baby for thirty to sixty minutes. The most common source of dehydration that we see in babies is from lack of milk. Whether mom is dead, sick, or injured the baby is unable to nurse. However, things such as hot weather, no water source, diarrhea from illness, or blood loss can also cause dehydration.

Dehydration signs:

- poor skin elasticity
- shrunken appearance especially around eyes
- lethargy
- dry mucus membranes
- fast but weak pulse

We often use "tenting" to check for dehydration and skin turgor. Dehydrated skin does not bounce back into place. Its stiff and remains in a tent shape for a period of time depending on the severity of the fluid loss. This is best done along the back, at the base of the neck, and in between the shoulders. Pull the skin gently upwards and see if it bounces back into shape quickly.

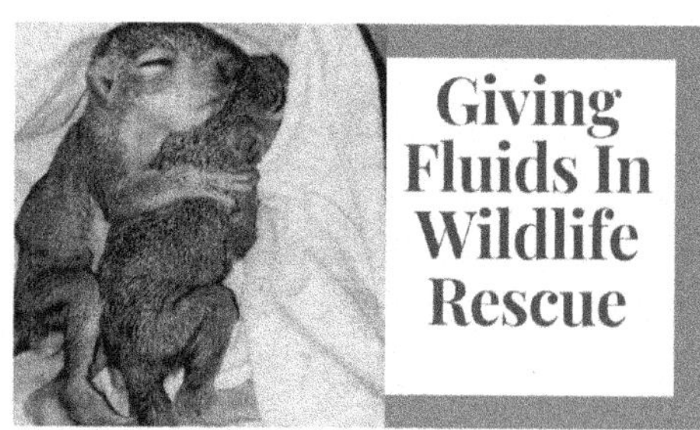

I have a YouTube video on giving fluids on my channel @foxruneec

Methods To Rehydrate
ORAL

There are several methods you can use to rehydrate. The method you use will depend on the health of the animal and the type of fluid you are using. The first is oral. This method works well if the baby is **conscious and alert**.

I typically go with an unflavored Pedialyte. This is commonly sold in drug stores and groceries. Fox Valley also carries an Electrolyte Replacer for Rehydration.

The unflavored Pedialyte can be hard to find so use flavored if you must. For the flavored kind you should split 50/50 with filtered water. This is because they contain a lot of sugar.
Do not use sports drinks - they contain too much sugar and salt for squirrels.

Using a syringe and a nipple you can give warm fluids via the mouth. For young babies, my nipples of choice are the Miracle Nipples. Very slowly drip some fluids into the mouth. Watch for the baby to swallow. Hold the syringe upwards at a 45 degree angle. (see pictures on next page)

Don't use the oral method if the animal is unconscious, has neurological symptoms, or is having seizures.

The baby must be warm before you can provide hydration. Do not rehydrate a cold baby.

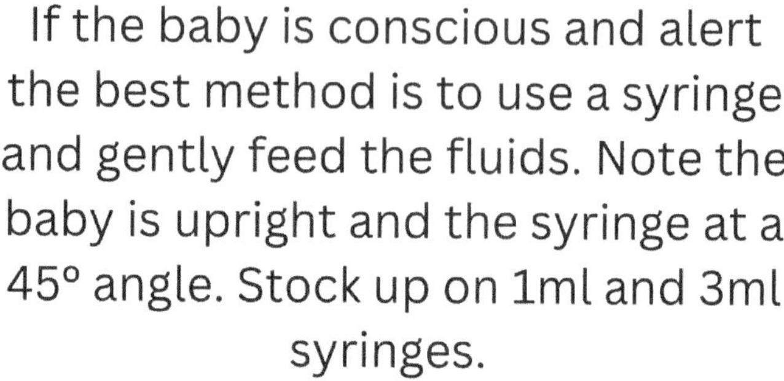

If the baby is conscious and alert the best method is to use a syringe and gently feed the fluids. Note the baby is upright and the syringe at a 45° angle. Stock up on 1ml and 3ml syringes.

If the baby is unconscious, uncooperative, or very dehydrated the best method is sub Q - inserting a needle under the skin and allow fluids to drip in. When the fluid builds up under the skin (marble size) stop giving fluids, let the animals body absorb the fluid, and if needed administer fluids again.

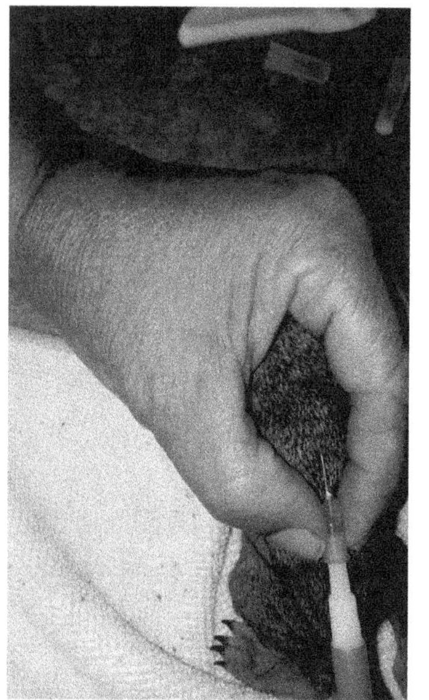

Photos by Ame Vanorio

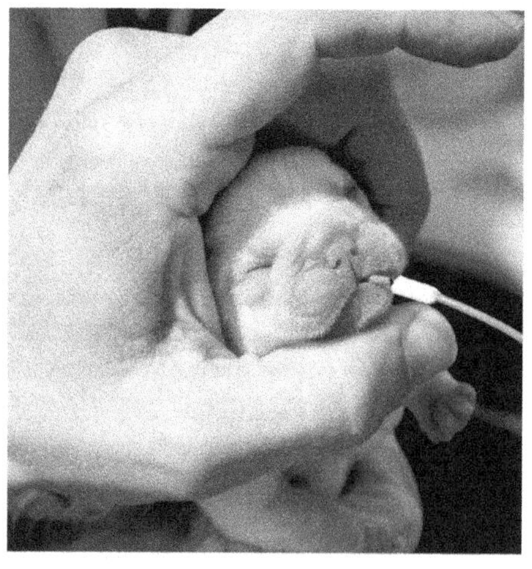

Photo by Den Guy

Tube feeding is another method where a tube is sent down the esophagus to stomach chamber. You should get trained by your veterinarian since this method can be medically tricky. I have only used it with opossums and find that squirrels typically don't need tube feeding. (Yes, that is a puppy)

Sub Q
Under the Skin

Subcutaneous means under the skin and is often referred to as SubQ. If an animal can not or will not take fluids orally then the subcutaneous method is the right option. This method is not quite as fast-acting because the fluids need to be absorbed by the body.

A needle is inserted just under the skin and the fluid is inserted via a syringe or a drip line. This is an easy technique to learn from a veterinarian or experienced wildlife rehabilitator.

For SubQ you can't use Pedialyte you need specially formulated solutions. Lactated Ringers is the brand most often used by veterinarians. It is an isotonic solution which means it will not draw fluid from the cells via osmosis.

IV solutions require a prescription. I typically buy the Ringers from my vet. You can also purchase from Chewy or KVSupply with a prescription from your vet. Plan on having one to three bags on hand depending on how many animals you take in.

It's important to keep in mind that this process can cause the animal discomfort and even pain. They may cry or make sounds of distress. Their skin is dry and tight and by giving sub Q fluids we are stretching the skin. Be sensitive and know that hydration will help!

If you have not given Sub-Q fluids before ask your vet or another wildlife rehabilitator to demonstrate for you.

Always use warm but never hot fluids. Never microwave fluids as it can cause pockets of high heat within the fluids.

Formula Feeding

Three very important notes:

1. Never give baby formula until they have been properly rehydrated
2. Formula is food. Yes, it's a liquid but it contains nutrients, fats, and protein that must be digested.
3. The transition to formula must be slow so the body can adapt.

Transitioning From Fluids To Formula

Once the Fox Valley formula arrives, (or you have acquired temporary puppy formula) gently transition from the fluids to formula over six feedings. This helps the baby to slowly transition to formula without stressing its immature and stressed digestive system.

First two feedings: Combine two parts hydration fluid with one part formula (2:1)

Second two feedings: Combine one part hydration mixture to one part formula (1:1)

Last two feedings: Combine one part fluids to two parts formula (1:2)

After that, you can move on to regular strength formula feedings. If you start with Esbilac and need to move to Fox Valley you should also transition slowly mixing the two formulas as above.

Baby ground squirrel.

What I recommend

Fox Valley Animal Nutrition manufactures formula for wildlife. Amazon and Henry's Pets are good places to order. This formula composite is made to meet the needs of growing squirrels. There are two types. 32/40 is for under 4 weeks and the 20/50 is for babies over 4 weeks old.

Esbilac Puppy Milk powder can be used **TEMPORARILY** as it does not have the complete nutrients needed for healthy growth. However, it is easy to find locally in a pinch. Order Fox Valley asap.

Wild animals have higher metabolisms and so have different nutrient requirements than your puppy or kitten. Talk to your veterinarian or an experienced wildlife rehabber to decide on a formula. Don't use social media as an authority for information.

Nursing ground squirrel

MASS MARKET FORMULAS TO AVOID

There are a number of formulas that have been produced for the puppy and kitten market that do not meet the needs of wildlife. Most Specialists say for squirrels **DO NOT USE** Condensed milk, cow milk, Hartz, human baby formula, kitten formula, Mothers Helper, Nurtural, or other like brands. They are made for other species and will not meet the nutritional needs of a squirrel. Nutritional-related problems such as MBD (see the Disease section) often take months to manifest themselves but originate with poor formula choices.

HOW MUCH FORMULA?

Every squirrel will vary but there is a basic rule of thumb. Weigh the baby using a gram scale. The stomach capacity is generally about 5% of the body weight.

Divide the total body weight by 5%.

For example, if a baby weighs 100 grams then 5% of that is 5ml's. We use cc's or ml's to measure the fluid. After you mix the formula you just draw up the correct amount into a syringe that nicely has the levels marked on it.

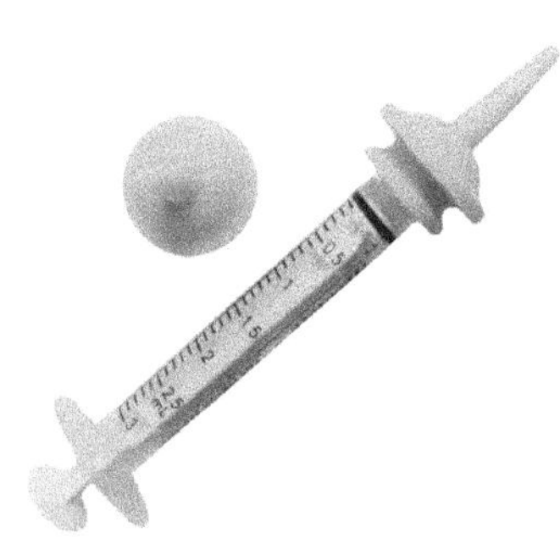

I use Miracle nipples. They were developed and patented by a squirrel wildlife rehabilitator! The "Mini" is a good size for young squirrels and then I bump up to the regular as they grow. Many people like catac nipples. An eyedropper can work in an emergency but get a syringe and appropriate nipple asap. I use 1 ml syringes for newborns.

Stock up on nipples and small syringes. Nipples do wear out and they get chewed on by teething babies. Wash them gently in between feedings.

How To Mix, Heat, and Store

Mix powdered formula with very warm water. If you are using Fox Valley it is one part dry formula to two parts water. Shake vigorously. The shakers they make for protein mixes or even a water bottle work. Allow it to sit for a few minutes to dissolve and shake again.

Never heat the formula in a microwave. It doesn't heat evenly and will have hot spots that burn the baby.

Microwave a mug or bowl of just water. Heat to nice and warm but not hot. Draw up the formula in the syringe and then place it in warm water. Also, baby bottle warmers can be useful.

Test it on your wrist before feeding (should be nice and warm). If the syringe formula cools during feeding then put it in the bowl of water to warm again.

Make formula in small batches and store in the fridge in between feedings. Discard the made-up formula after 24 hours.

WHAT ARE CC'S AND ML'S?

CC stands for cubic centimeter. ML stands for millimeter. They are just two ways that are used to measure volume in the metric system.

CC and ML are interchangeable. When you look at your syringe you want to pay attention to the number – not whether your unit says cc or ml.

syringes can be purchased online or at local farm stores. For squirrels get small ones that are one cc or 1 ml. Make sure that the fractions are marked.

Use a kitchen gram scale to weigh each baby. Then multiply that number by 5% (.05) and that will be the number of cc's (or ml's) to feed per feeding. You may need to start with smaller feedings at first, especially on thin babies, and work up to 5%.

As They Grow Ask Yourself:

- Are they gaining weight steadily? Weigh them every couple of days when they are small and record the data.
- Are they active and exploring at an age-appropriate level?
- Do they appear sick or weak?

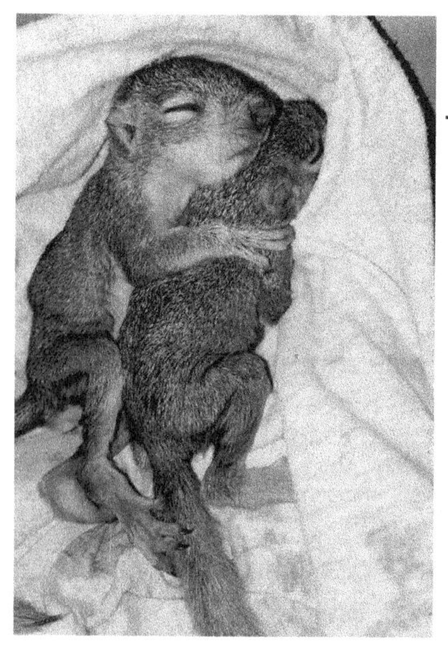

These two came into my center very dehydrated and emaciated. So if they look poorly to you - then good call because they were in bad shape. Time was good and they both matured healthy and strong!
Photo credit: Ame Vanorio

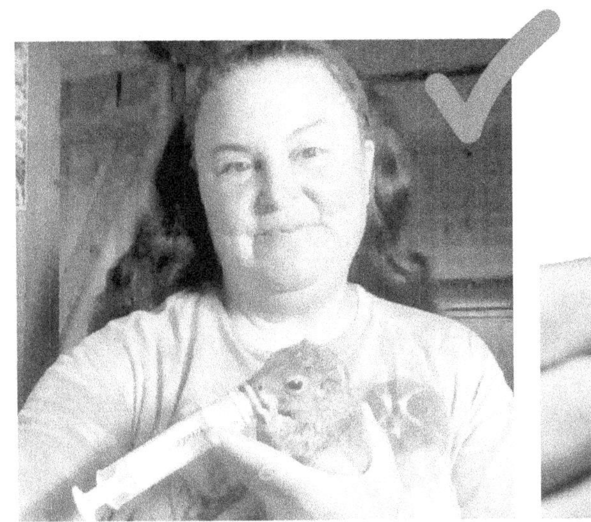

The two pictures above show me
feeding a squirrel properly.
Squirrel upright with syringe at 45°

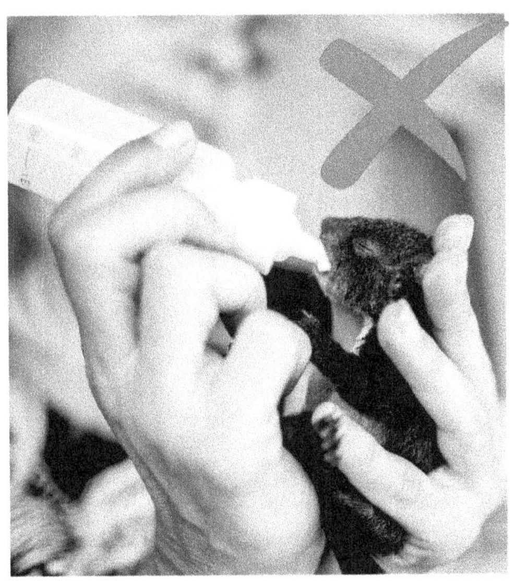

Never use pet nursers or doll bottles. The fluids flow to fast and can aspirate the baby. Aspiration is when fluids or formula enters the lungs. This can cause infection.

Don't turn the bottle so that it is facing down. This causes the formula to run faster into their mouth and the baby can choke.
Feed in a quiet environment.

If fluids comes out of babies mouth or nose, then stop. You are going too fast. Gently turn the baby's head down while supporting body and allow fluid to come out. Then wipe his nose and mouth with a tissue. A human infant aspirator bulb can also be used.
Start over, slower. Allow them time to swallow. Babies can aspirate causing pneumonia, which can be fatal unless treated with medicine. Use a small syringe not more than 1cc for neonates so that it releases a small amount. Baby squirrels have a small esophagus!

Feeding Baby Flying Squirrels and Chipmunks

Flying squirrels and chipmunks are quite as small as neonates and may need some specialized equipment to feed them.

For babies under 12 grams syringe cannulas can be used to feed them formula. The cannula helps control the flow of milk or formula, ensuring that the baby squirrel receives an appropriate amount of nourishment without the risk of aspiration (inhaling the liquid into the lungs). Syringe cannulas allow for precise control over the amount of fluid or medication being administered, which is important for the small and delicate systems of these squirrels.

 Carol Hardee, B.S., M.S., Director of Wildlife Rehabilitation Center of Central Florida states that she does this for these little guys "After heating a small, white cannula (the larger end) with a lit match, I push it firmly onto the end of a ½ ml O-ring syringe".

After they are above 12 grams she switches to a Catac nipple. Another method that is often used with mice is to dip a small watercolor paintbrush in the formula and put it at the tip of the mouth. This can help to transition them to a nipple. Make sure you have plenty of small syringes of 1 ml.

Flying Squirrel (left) and Chipmunk (right)   Catac nipples

Charts: Formula Feeding and Physical Milestones

*** These are guidelines and represent averages. Make sure to weigh your squirrels several times a week to make sure they are gaining weight. Double check amounts of formula using the 5% rule. You know your squirrels best. If you feel they are struggling contact your veterinarian.

Gray Squirrels

Age	Weight/grams	Amount Per Feeding	How Often/ Formula	Night Feeding	Behaviors/Appearance
Birth	10 – 20 grams	.5 1.0ml	Every 2 – 2.5 hours during the day	Two nighttime feedings	Born pink with no fur, eyes, and ears closed. Ears flat against head. No teeth.
One Week	20 – 40 grams	1.0 – 2.0 ml	Every 2.0 – 2.5 hours	One to Two nighttime feedings	Umbilical cord falls off. They begin making sounds. Soft grey coat starts to grow. Ears start to stick up.
Two Weeks	40 – 60 grams	2 – 3.0ml	Feed every 3.5 hours	One nighttime feeding	Skin darkens as the baby coat grows. Eyes still closed but they can hear. Front teeth emerge.
Three Weeks	60 – 80 grams	3 – 4.0ml	Feed six times per day including one night feeding	One	Their eyes may open (sometimes one at a time on different days)
Four Weeks	80 – 120 grams	4 – 6ml		Discontinue the nighttime feeding	They will start to walk, unsteadily at first. Tail still straight.
Five Weeks	120 – 140 grams	6 -7ml	4 – 5 times a day	0	Tail begins to look furry. They are beginning to eat solid food. See page on weaning foods. Beginning to play and climb.
Six Weeks	140 – 160 grams	7 – 8ml	3 – 4 times a day	0	Move them to a larger grow-out cage and give them opportunities to climb. They will start to hold foods. Give pieces of rodent/squirrel block. Have a water bottle.

Gray Squirrels cont.

Age	Weight/grams	Amount Per Feeding	How Often/ formula	Night Feeding	Behaviors/Appearance
7 – 8 weeks	170 -250 grams	8.5 – 12ml	3 times a day	0	They should be sitting up on their haunches, tails are curling, and they enjoy playing.
8 – 9 weeks	260 - 380	12.5 – 19 ml	2 times a day	0	You should be offering a variety of weaning foods. Tail is bushy. They are starting to show independence and look more like adults. You can formula feed through the cage if they do not want to be held.
10 – 12 weeks	400 - 600 grams	20 ml	2 times per day	0	Depending on the weather they need to move to an outside grow-out cage so they can adapt to outside smells and sounds. Give them plenty of opportunities to climb, hide, and toys to play with. Offer weaning foods early morning and evening.
13 – 14 weeks		20ml	1 time per day	0	They are about ¾ of their adult size.
					Release! See the release criteria.

Flying Squirrels

Age	Weight/grams	Amount Per Feeding	How Often/ Formula	Nights	Behaviors/Appearance
Birth	3-6 grams	.15 - .3ml	Feed every two hours.	Two nighttime feedings	Born pink with no fur, eyes, and ears closed. No teeth. 2.5 inches long. Born with patagium (extra skin for gliding)
One Week	8 grams	.4ml	Feed every two hours	2	Fur growing on head
Two Weeks	10-15 grams	.5 - .75ml		One nighttime feeding	Lower incisors erupt
Three Weeks	15 – 20 grams	.75 – 1.0ml	Feed every three hours	1	Ears open
Four Weeks	25 grams	1.25ml	Every three hours.	Stop nighttime feeding	Eyes open
Five Weeks	30 grams	1.5ml	Feed every four hours	0	Fully furred. They start to play. Flyers are very social and like to play together. Start to offer weaning foods. Give water bottle.
Six Weeks	35 grams	1.75 ml	Formula feed every 5 hours	0	Eating solid foods in addition to formula.

Flying Squirrels cont.

Age	Weight/grams	Amount Per Feeding	How Often/ Formula	Nights	Behaviors/Appearance
7 weeks	42 grams	2.1 ml	Formula feed every 6 hours	0	They should be ready for a large grow-out cage that provides enough room for them to practice gliding. They enjoy toys and a nest box.
8 – 10 weeks	46 – 52 grams	2.3 – 2.6 ml	Formula feed 2 times a day		They are eating weaning foods and have access to a water bottle. They can jump 2-3 feet and need to practice that.
10 – 12 weeks	52 – 58 grams	2.6 – 2.9 ml	Wean from formula – provide antlers or cuttlebone for minerals		Flying squirrels molt at around 12 weeks.
12 – 14 weeks	58 – 62 grams				Place insects in leaf litter in the enclosure for them to find.
Release			It is beneficial to release them in the vicinity of other flyers. Take their nest box with them and place it in a tree in their new location.		Flying squirrels are nocturnal. Help them to adjust to a nocturnal schedule if they are not doing it naturally.

Chipmunks

Age	Weight/ Grams	Amount	How Often/ Formula	Nights	Behaviors Appearance
Birth	2.5 – 3 grams	.05 - .1 ml	Feed every 2 hours	1	Born furless, ears, and eyes closed.
1 week	4 – 8 grams	0.2 – 0.4 ml	Feed every three hours	1	Stripes begin to show and fur starts to grow. Lower front teeth erupt.
2 weeks	20 g	1 ml	Feed every 4 hours	1	Mostly furred but can not thermoregulate yet.
3 weeks	30g	1.5 ml	Feed every 5 hours	0	Ears open, fully furred with stripes visible. Top front teeth erupt. Start offering weaning foods.
4 weeks	40g	2 ml	Formula feed 3 times per day	0	Eyes open. They should be getting a variety of weaning foods (offer them one at a time) They should be active. Add a water bottle.
5 weeks	60 grams	3 ml	2 X per day	0	Continue weaning foods adding foods found in their natural diet. Put in a pre-release enclosure outside.
6 - 8 weeks	70 grams		0	0	Weaned. Reduce human contact. Continue to offer weaning and natural foods. Hide food in the sand and leaf litter at bottom of the enclosure.
9 – 10 weeks	80 grams				Release. See release criteria.

Weaning Foods

Baby squirrels can start nibbling at foods shortly after opening their eyes. Don't cut back on formula! That is still their main source of nutrition until they are 14 weeks old.

Make slow changes to diet. I am a big fan of human baby foods as a first food. In particular sweet potatoes because they are nutrient-dense.

Many wildlife rehabilitators would not agree. In part because it's messy and the baby may need a sponge bath. (Don't immerse in water) Also, the argument can be made that baby squirrels don't get pureed foods in nature. I would argue that baby food makes a good transition food.

In addition, I sometimes mix in 1/8 teaspoon of calcium carbonate in the baby food and mix in. Calcium is very important for squirrels. Rodent chow is a good foundation food for weaning.

Natural Foods

Start adding in foods on this list as they grow. Only introduce one new food at a time. Squirrels can be picky and need to get used to new foods.

Tree Squirrels

Cambium - this is that soft layer under the bark of trees.
Caterpillars - from your organic garden
Egg - an occasional hard boiled egg. Yes, they eat them raw in nature but store eggs can contain pathogens when uncooked.
Fungus - mushrooms, fungi growing on trees, and mosses
Fruit - small quantities of berries, apples, pears
Nuts - acorns, beech, hickory, spruce, also pumpkin seeds
Small branches & twigs - mulberry (a favorite at my house), maple, sweet gum. Tree buds from mulberry and fruit trees were always a favorite in spring. Catkins from oaks and helicopters from maples are enjoyed.

Flying Squirrels

Flying squirrels like mushrooms and other fungi and will dig for truffles. They eat tree products similar to other tree squirrels.

They eat more insects than other tree squirrels. Check out pet stores and bait stores for earthworms, live or freeze-dried crickets and mealworms. An occasional hard boiled egg will help with protein needs.

Ground Squirrels and Chipmunks

They eat much of the same thing as tree squirrels. However, both will dig and eat tender roots and bulbs. They also enjoy snail, insects, and worms. It helps them to learn digging skills if you bury the insects and worms in a pan of soil and let them "hunt". They will also eat more flowers such as dandelion and Queen Anne's Lace as well as grass seeds such as wheat grass and brome grass seeds.

Minerals

All squirrels need access to minerals. Deer and elk antlers provide needed minerals and help keep the squirrels teeth trimmed. They gnaw on them in the wild. You can order antlers online or go to a local pet store. Just make sure you get untreated ones. You can also place cuttlebones in their enclosures. Cuttlebones are sold at pet stores as a mineral supplement for birds.

Squirrels will also occasionally eat soil for the mineral content. Specifically, sodium, calcium and magnesium, which are lacking in the seeds and nuts they eat (Grant, 2009).

Supplements

Ame's soapbox!! I do believe that supplements can play an important role in the health of your squirrel. And as an organic farmer and herbal practitioner I do believe in herbal medicine. BUT there is definitely a time and a place. In addition, I believe each situation is unique. You need to consider the squirrels health needs, consult with your veterinarian and make an informed decision. That said here are some supplements I have found beneficial.

Pumpkin and applesauce are great sources of fiber. Yes, these are foods but in this instance we are using them for a specific purpose. They can help move bowels in an older baby. I am a big fan of feeding both as part of a balanced diet in the weaning and grow out phases as they are high in vitamins and antioxidants. Applesauce should be unsweetened and limited to half a teaspoon a day.

Probiotics

Bene-Bac Plus Pet Gel Probiotics is a product I have had good success with. Contains live, naturally occurring digestive microorganisms. It's available from Amazon and Henrys and many local pet stores. Bene Bac is beneficial with squirrels who are taking antibiotics, recovering from illness or injury, or under stress.

L-Lysine

L-lysine is an essential amino acid that some tree-dwelling squirrels may be deficient in. A deficiency may inhibit them from absorbing calcium. L-lysine (Lys) is an essential amino acid is recommended for many diseases such as squirrel pox and helps optimize animal growth or increase milk production in nursing mothers. L-lysine sulfate and L-lysine HCl are considered safe for all animal species when supplemented in appropriate amounts.

Calcium Carbonate Powder

Squirrels have a high need for calcium. A healthy squirrel eating a quality diet does not need supplemental calcium. A squirrel that is ill, has spinal damage, and/or has Metabolic Bone disease needs extra calcium in their diet. You can purchase Calcium Carbonate Powder to sprinkle on their food or mix with formula. I will talk about MBD in the disease section.

B & C Vitamins

B Vitamins can be beneficial for short term use. They help stimulate appetite and can help with healing. Vitamin C is good for wound healing.

Multi Vitamins

I never give multi vitamins for a long period time. Again a healthy diet for a heathy squirrel doesn't need a general multi-vitamin. The fat soluble vitamins such as A and E can build up to dangerous level. However, a squirrel that is compromised may benefit from a short term vitamin dose.

DO NOT FEED:

- Chocolate
- Avocado
- Grapes and raisins
- Onions and garlic
- Bird food
- Bread, crackers, chips
- Sugary Cereal
- Candy

These foods are bad for squirrels

Teething

Just like in human babies, teething can cause discomfort. This can cause them to not nurse or eat or can make them want to gnaw things. The chart below is for gray squirrels. Be patient and make sure they have rodent block and some fresh twigs. Keep offering formula.

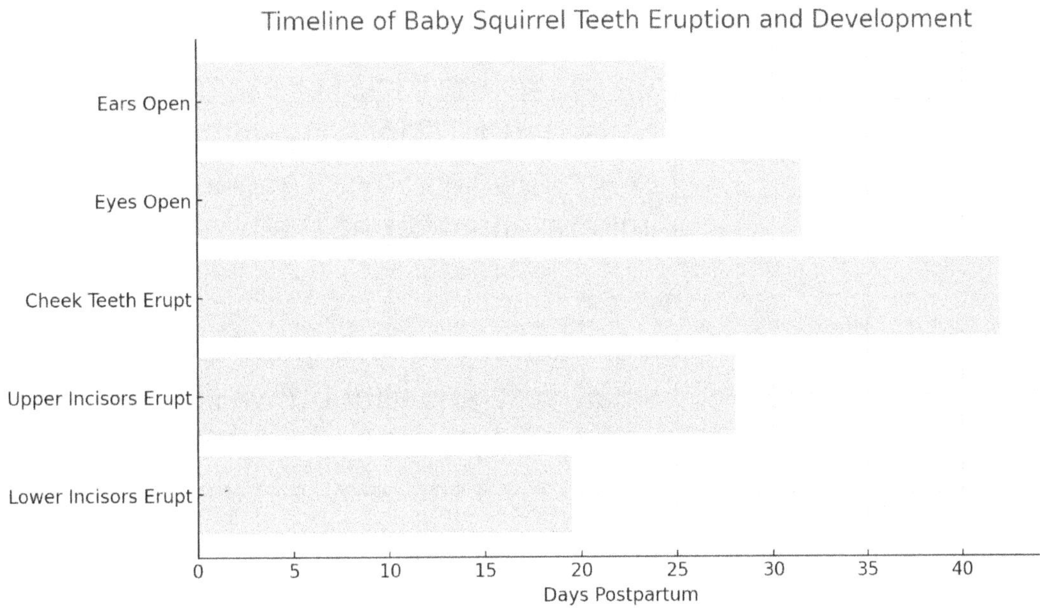

Poop and Pee

Be prepared to be totally riveted by how much your squirrel poops and pees!

A small baby with eyes closed will need stimulation to poop and pee. You do this by swiping something over the genitals. A warm baby wipes, moist cotton ball, or Q-tip can do the trick. For example, with boys start a 1/2 inch above the penis and swipe down and over the penis. This imitates mom licking them.

Normal baby squirrel poop is typically small, soft, and light brown in color. The consistency can be somewhat pasty, especially if the baby is still nursing and consuming milk. As the squirrel starts eating more solid foods, the poop may become firmer and darker.

It's important to monitor the poop for any changes in color, consistency, or frequency, as these can indicate health issues.

Baby squirrels may develop diarrhea if they are ill and also if they overeat. These babies need to go back to fluids for one or two feedings. More in the Problems section.

Penis Problems

A warning about penises! Squirrels naturally want to suck and sometimes the boy's penis becomes a pacifier. (photo at top)

The penis will become red and swollen which may interfere with their peeing. This can be painful.

I typically separate them out for a few days to allow healing. Apply Neosporin to help with healing. You can also place a sock with the toes cut off as a kind of skirt to protect the penis.

In addition, place some toys, nuts, and twigs in the enclosure to occupy their mouths. I have tried placing a band-aid over the penis with mixed results. Watch to make sure they don't chew the bandage.

And just to clarify.
Genital nursing does occur to females as well resulting in red and irritated vulvas. Separate and treat like the boys.

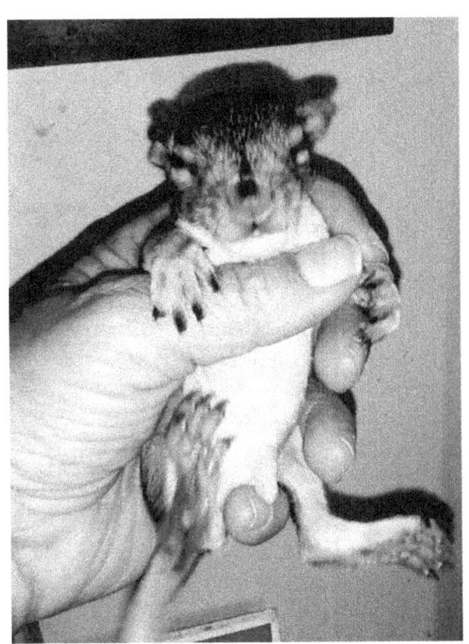

The bottom picture shows a normal penis.
Photo by Ame Vanorio

Squirrel Pests and Diseases

Volume 2 in my series **Diseases & Parasites in Wildlife Rehabilitation** covers problems in general. Here I am going to look at them again but talk about the ones that apply to squirrels and squirrel specific treatments.

Squirrels get a number of pests and diseases. some are easy to manage and some take more time (and money). It's important to give your new intake(s) a thorough exam to look for symptoms and signs of problems.

Zoonotic diseases or zoonoses are diseases that can be transferred from animal to human or from human to animal. As wildlife rehabilitators, we need to be aware of them as many are potentially dangerous.

Rabies is probably the most famous zoonotic disease. Fortunately, squirrels rarely get rabies. The Wisconsin Department of Health states that "Small rodents (e.g., squirrels, hamsters, guinea pigs, gerbils, chipmunks, rats, and mice) and lagomorphs (rabbits and hares), whether wild or kept as pets, are rarely found to be infected with rabies and have not been known to transmit rabies to humans". I do not vaccinate squirrels for rabies. However, I do recommend all wildlife rehabilitators get the Rabies Pre-exposure Prophylaxis shots.

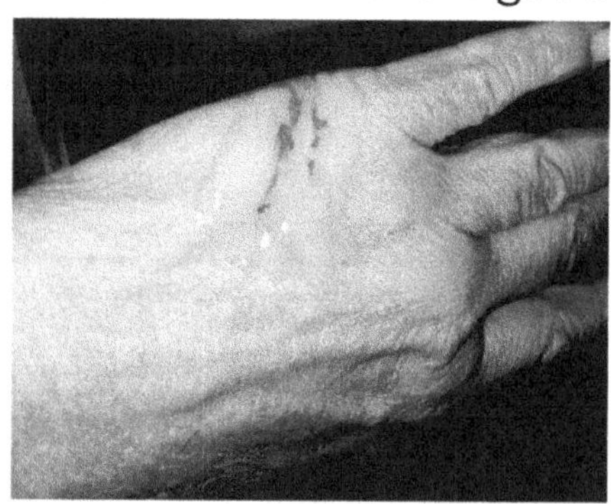

Keep in mind that anytime you are working with wildlife you should take precautions such as frequent hand washing and wearing latex or vinyl gloves. Also leather gloves are good. All animals can and do bite. Here's my hand after a squirrel attack :)

External Parasites

 External parasites live on the outside of the animal's body. You may see their eggs, fecal matter, or bodies during an exam. These external parasites are often seen on baby wildlife.

It's common for baby squirrels to have fleas and lice. If they have wounds then maggots are likely as well. I don't see as many ticks on squirrels but look carefully, especially on babies who have fallen from the nest and are on the ground.

The good thing about external pests is that you can see and identify the adult quite easily. Nymphs and larval stages are small and you may need a magnifying lens. Treatments are often easy to apply and purchase.

The challenge with external pests is that they are prolific, and it may take repeated treatments to get them under control. Ticks and fleas have both been found in Antarctica where they feed on northern birds such as penguins.

Also, if you are not careful and diligent, they can easily spread throughout your home. Have an examination area such as a countertop or stainless steel table. An area you can disinfect and clean easily. Don't pick up a new arrival and hold it against your chest. That is just inviting the parasites to climb on you.

Orphaned baby wildlife is prone to parasites because they have not had a mother to groom them. A heavy load of external parasites may result in anemia, weakness, and secondary skin infections. So treating them ASAP is important.

Removing External Parasites

I am all in favor of treating pests naturally as I was a certified organic farmer for many years. However, we need to consider the number of parasites on the baby, the size of the litter, and other factors that may be compromising their health.

For compromised squirrels, I start with a chemical treatment and then use a natural treatment to control the pests. This is because I need something that will act quickly to help stabilize their health. Natural products are great, but they don't often kill the parasite quickly thus eliminating the issue. In some cases, time is essential to save the life of the animal.

Non-chemical ways

• Keep incoming squirrels in a quarantine area away from other animals to avoid transmission.

• Apply insect repellent to your clothes so they don't get on your body and use you as a transportation mode.

• Change bedding frequently. Don't leave infected bedding lying around. Place in a sealed garbage bag to either launder (hot water and high dry) or toss out.

For laundering fleas and lice, the Center for Disease Control (CDC) recommends temperatures greater than 128.3 F for ten minutes.

• I also have washed bedding in flea and tick shampoo to assist with destroying any that is on the bedding. Double rinse!

• Ticks and maggots may be easy to pick off by hand. Use tweezers or a special tick-removal tool.

• The CDC recommends using tweezers to grab the tick as close to the skin as possible. Pull upwards without twisting. Don't squish the tick because that can spread disease through body fluids.

• Flea and lice combs are also useful to remove them and then dunk in soapy water.

• Fleas can sometimes be removed by using a lint roller or masking tape to catch them. This can work well in an infant that hasn't grown fur yet.

- Products that are made for domestic animals can be used for wildlife. Caution is needed to use the correct dosage and type of treatment per species. The best is to find products developed for pet rats. Puppy and kitten are next best and milder.
- A bath can be given using an insecticide soap made for kittens or puppies. Use caution because this may cause undue stress to squirrels and cause further compilations.
- For neonate or compromised squirrels put the powder or spray on a cloth and then gently wipe it on the body. Don't spray chemicals or put topicals on infants.
- Use products with plant-based and natural ingredients. Vet's Best has a line of natural flea and tick repellants. Keep in mind that natural ingredients can still be strong so look for products ok for kittens or pet rats.
- Don't use Revolution®, Stronghold® (generic Selamectin) or Advantage® topical treatments unless under the guidance of a vet. A dosage that is too strong can be harmful. Squirrel bodies are tiny and many of these drugs were made for larger species.

Maggots

Maggots are fly eggs. The fly's lay the eggs on exposed flesh such as a wound. When the eggs hatch the larvae (worms) will eat the squirrels flesh. Clean the wound with saline solution (I will cover more in the wound section) and pick out the fly eggs and larvae.

Capstar® (Nitenpyram) is an over the counter treatment that kills maggots as well as fleas. It is easy to find on Amazon or Henry's Pets. For young squirrels I prefer to grind up 1/2 tablet and mix it with 2 mL of warm water. After it dissolves spray it on the squirrel avoiding the eyes and mouth. You can also divide the pill and mix 1/4 pill (one fourth) with 1mL warm water in a syringe and give orally. Capstar also works on fleas!

Mange/Mites

There are several types of mites. Mites are common in ears and under the skin. They are ridiculously small, and some are microscopic.
Mites are arachnids that burrow under the skin. They reproduce rapidly and can also infect bedding and cages.

MANGE

The most severe mites that I see are mange.
Mange causes several symptoms:

- Severe itching
- Skin that is scaly, and irritated looking
- Distinct bad smell from dead skin and infection
- Hair loss especially face, legs and groin
- Severe causes leave crusty lesions on the body
- Swelling especially around eyes

Mange is serious. The symptoms can become so bad that the animal can't look for food and begins to starve to death. This is when you will get phone calls. These animals are hungry and start coming into people's yards looking for food or help.

You can check for mites by viewing a skin scraping under a 4X setting on a microscope. There are two types of mange mites that typically effect fox and gray squirrels. Notoedres douglasi (Notoedric mange) or Sarcoptes scabiei (Sarcoptic mange).

The mites typically start around the head and can spread to the entire body in a matter of weeks. By the time you see the squirrel they have most likely been infected for several months.
The entire mite life cycle is spent on the host and lasts about 21 days. It is transmitted by direct contact and the young often get it from the parent.

CLEAN AND ISOLATE

Mange is very contagious and will spread to other animals in your care. In addition, humans can get mites. They can not reproduce on your body, but they can dig in and chew on your skin. This will cause intense itching and pain.

• Keep the animal with mange in isolation.
• Wear gloves when you treat, feed, or clean the mange animal. Wear protective clothing and insect repellent because while they don't live on humans they will bite you.
• Bedding should be changed daily, placed in a sealed garbage bag, and thrown out.

While not squirrels this gives you an idea of what mange looks like.

Lice

APPLE CIDER VINEGAR

While it won't kill adult lice, apple cider vinegar will cause the nits protective coating to break down killing these eggs. Then use a lice comb to remove the nits.

Use caution on infants because vinegar is acidic and can irritate the skin. Swab nits with a cotton ball or Q-Tip soaked in apple cider vinegar.

Fleas

Fleas are smaller than ticks and hop as their mode of locomotion. You may see pepper-like flecks on the skin which are flea feces. The larvae feed on these feces.

Fleas and small mites are common when baby squirrels first come from the nest. If the squirrel is furless, a warm bath with a couple of drops of Dawn Dishwashing Liquid will take care of the problem. If the baby has fur, you'll need to use a flea killer. I recommend using kitten flea powder, as it is usually safe for squirrels too.

When treating, don't put the powder directly on the squirrel. Instead, place a paper towel at the bottom of a container, sprinkle the flea powder on the towel, and then cover it with another paper towel. Finally, place the squirrel on top of this setup. This method helps avoid getting too much powder on the squirrel's skin or fur and prevents them from breathing it in. Cover the squirrel lightly with fleece to keep it warm and monitor it closely.
You can use gentle sprays for birds. To use this, spray a cloth and gently rub the squirrel with it. Never spray the squirrel directly.

Important note: Beware of using harsh commercial products. Buy products from your vet, pet store, or a reliable brand. Many products sold at big box stores are produced in China or India and contain strong chemicals that can kill baby animals.

The

Flea

For young squirrels I prefer to grind up 1/2 tablet of Capstar and mix it with 2 mL of warm water. After it dissolves spray it on the squirrel avoiding the eyes and mouth. You can also divide the pill and mix 1/4 pill (one fourth) with 1mL warm water in a syringe and give orally.

Tree Squirrel Bot Fly, *Cuterebra emasculator*

The tree squirrel bot fly or warble fly, is a more unusual pest that affects squirrels and chipmunks in Eastern North America. They are especially common in the southeast.

The botfly lays its eggs on plants, and the squirrel breathes in the eggs. Inside their lungs, the eggs hatch into larvae and then move to areas under the skin. As they grow, you can see a lump forming, which soon develops a breathing hole. If left alone, the lump will become very large and oval-shaped. In late summer you can see the large swollen skin sacks that are caused by the growing larvae.

Use tweezers to remove the bots from the sack. (Gross I know!) Then clean the affected skin and apply first aid cream. Not many studies have been done on effective treatments but talk to your vet if they look severe.

Eastern gray squirrel with swollen skin wounds caused by the tree squirrel bot fly.

Internal Parasites

There are several worming medicines available and some work better than others on certain worm species. Also, some wormers are quite strong, and care should be taken with young, compromised bodies.

Worming doses are very small so this is the time to use those 1ml syringes. That way you can measure accurately. check with your vet for their recommendations.

My go-to wormer is Pyrantel Pamoate® Suspension because it is low-risk and treats a number of species of parasites, especially hookworm and roundworm. Dose is 1ml/2 pounds so for a squirrel that weighs 225 grams they would receive @ .25ml

Fenbendazole (Panacur® & Safe-Guard®) is also considered safe for squirrels. Works well on hookworm, tapeworm, roundworm, and whipworm. Typically dosed at 3 mg per 1000 grams weight.

I know rehabbers that use Ivermectin. I am not a fan of Ivermectin for wildlife. After having two bad experiences I stopped using it. Talk to your veterinarian to decide what medications you will use.

Wounds

Wounds need to be cleaned and treated. I use chlorohexidine. A solution of 1 % Chlorhexidine or Betadine. I draw it up in a syringe and flush the wounds and apply a dressing as needed. Deep gashes may require stitches.

Abscesses

Abscesses are often caused by a cat bite or other animal attacking the squirrel. They look like a swelling or lump and are full of pus. The mouth of the attacking animal contains bacteria. You should consult with your veterinarian to discuss treatment. Abscesses often require antibiotics. They also may need to be punctured, drained, and cleaned. Applying a warm compress can help it drain.

Antibiotics may be needed to deal with wounds, infections and diseases. Antibiotics can often cause digestive problems and diarrhea so extra fluids and probiotics are helpful.

Baytril and Sulfamethoxazole are considered safe for rodents.

Clavamox is a form of Augmentin that is often used in wildlife and is often prescribed for pneumonia and wound infections. It is frequently prescribed after cat bites. Not all rehabbers feel this is a safe drug for squirrels so consult with your vet.

Debridement

Debridement is the removal of damaged tissue or foreign objects from a wound. Dead or necrotic tissue is often present in an older wound. When you remove the dead tissue it allows new healthy tissue to grow again. You can use small surgical scissors and surgical scrub to remove dead tissue.

Degloving

Degloving is when the skin and often deeper tissues are separated from the body. These incidents can occur when the victim is attacked by another animal or in a mechanical injury. The skin is basically ripped off the body. In squirrels, this can happen on any part of the body. However, the end of the tail is often degloved in an attempt to get away from a predator.

The degloved animal is often in shock. Any bleeding should be controlled first and then the wound needs to be cleaned with a sterile saline solution. One option is to apply topical silver sulfadiazine (also great for burns). Silver sulfadiazine is a prescription drug. Another option is Neosporin but it may not have the strength needed for a more severe case.

Bandage and wrap the area. Give Metacam for pain and inflammation.

Gunshot Wounds

Sadly, wildlife rehabilitators do receive animals that are shot in an effort to get rid of a nuisance animal or used for target practice.

Bullets and BB's push hair and dirt into the body often leading to infections. Depending on the bullet the squirrel may have bone, muscle, and/or vascular damage. They should be treated as open wounds. Merck Veterinary Manual suggest that they should not be closed up immediately since the risk of contamination is so high.

If a shot animal is 'out of season' or on the endangered species list take photos, save the bullet fragments, and immediately report it to your local Fish and Wildlife officer.

Back Injuries

I have taken in three adult squirrels that had back injuries due to falls. Honestly I have been amazed at the resilience of squirrels and how they will recover. Metacam (meloxicam) is a great drug and anti-inflammatory that reduces swelling . Spinal injuries are a wait and see type and I did collaborate with my vet because I don't want to prolong agony for them. But giving them time to heal is important. That and a warm, quiet, dark place.

Adults that come into your care may need to be given fluids like any other intake. In addition, they may be in shock and feel chilled. So place a heating pad partially under the cage. This can be tricky because with a spinal injury they may not be mobile. They may not have much interest in food but often I offer half strength formula in a syringe. I want them to get some nutrients but still go easy on there system. After a day or so as they feel better Ill offer some soft foods such as baked sweet potatoes and cooked broccoli.

If they come back from the
vet looking like this, they
feel better!!!
Photo: Ame Vanorio

Diseases

I will list some of the more common illnesses that you may encounter while rescuing and raising baby squirrels.

Fibromatosis aka Squirrel Pox

This is a nasty disease that unfortunately has no cure. It's a viral disease caused by the Lepripox virus causing large, wart-like tumors called fibromas. The fibromas can sometimes become ulcerated and infected with bacteria, leading to additional health issues. Humans do not get this virus.

It has been found in red, gray, and fox squirrels throughout the eastern and Midwest states and is a problem in the UK among Red Squirrels. It's transmitted by the bite of mosquitoes, fleas, or contact with infected squirrels.

Infected squirrels might show signs of discomfort, reduced mobility, or changes in behavior due to the tumors.

There is no specific treatment for squirrel fibromatosis, but here are some steps to manage the condition:

1. Supportive Care: Ensure the squirrel has a safe, stress-free environment with soft bedding. Soft foods or chow soaked in water since they can get pox on the inside of their mouth.
2. Monitor for Secondary Infections: Keep an eye on the fibromas for any signs of secondary bacterial infections. If you notice swelling, pus, or other signs of infection, it may be necessary to provide antibiotics.
3. Isolation: If you are caring for multiple squirrels, isolate the infected one to prevent the spread of the virus.
4. Some squirrels recover however in severe cases euthanasia may be the humane option.

I tried a couple of more unorthodox treatments. One was to give a bath in Aveno oatmeal bath treatment to relieve itching. The squirrel did not appreciate the bath! I have also given children's Benadryl® to help at the suggestion of another rehabber.
0.3ml twice daily. I do think there is value in giving a vitamin supplement for a short time to support the immune system.

West Nile Virus

West Nile Virus (WNV) is primarily known for affecting birds, humans, and horses, but it can also infect other animals, including squirrels. The primary mode of transmission for WNV is through the bite of an infected mosquito. Infected squirrels might show signs of neurological issues such as tremors, lack of coordination, difficulty moving, and weakness.

Supportive care is needed. Hydration and tube feeding may be necessary if the squirrel is having a hard time swallowing. NSAIDs such as Metacam are helpful. Create a quiet, stress-free environment. A warm, comfortable, and safe enclosure is essential for recovery. Avoid loud noises and excessive handling.

There is no cure but most animals make a full recovery. Some may display permanent neurological symptoms.
West Nile is transmitted by mosquitos so reducing their numbers around your home or center is smart. Change outside water dishes frequently and don't allow standing water to accumulate. Mosquitoes lay their eggs in moist soil and water and they typically hatch in 48 hours.

Metabolic Bone Disease

If you walk away from this book with any knowledge I hope it's that proper feeding of young squirrels is critical. Problems stemming from nutrition mistakes can rear their ugly heads months later. Squirrels and other rodents have a high need for calcium in their diets.

Metabolic Bone Disease (MBD) is one of those problems. MBD is a condition resulting from an imbalance of calcium, phosphorus, and vitamin D3 in their diet. It primarily affects captive squirrels or those in rehabilitation due to inadequate nutrition. This disease is totally preventable and curable in most cases but sometimes has permanent bone curvature requiring a forever home.

Causes:
- Calcium Deficiency: Lack of sufficient calcium in the diet.
- Phosphorus Imbalance: An excess of phosphorus relative to calcium can disrupt the balance necessary for healthy bone development and cause blood calcium levels to fall.
- Vitamin D3 Deficiency: Vitamin D3 is crucial for calcium absorption in the body. Lack of sunlight or dietary sources of vitamin D3 can lead to deficiencies.
- Starvation
- Weaning to early. Just because the young squirrel "looks" full grown doesn't mean they are ready to be weaned from formula. Keep feeding formula till 14 weeks.

Kitten Fur Syndrome (KFS) is a colloquial term sometimes used to describe the appearance of young squirrels that exhibit thin, fine fur and weak muscle development due to nutritional deficiencies, particularly protein and essential vitamins and minerals.

While MBD and KFS are not the same condition, they can be related in that both can result from inadequate nutrition. A young squirrel with KFS might also develop MBD if its diet lacks sufficient calcium and vitamin D3, leading to further complications with bone health.

MBD Con't.

Symptoms:
- Weakness and Lethargy: Affected squirrels may appear weak and lethargic.
- Bone Deformities: Softening of bones (osteomalacia) can lead to deformities, fractures, and abnormal bone growth.
- Lameness and Difficulty Moving: Squirrels may have difficulty walking, climbing, or moving due to weakened bones. Drags hind legs.
- Tremors and Muscle Twitching: Neurological symptoms such as tremors and muscle twitching can occur due to calcium imbalances affecting nerve function.
- Swollen Joints: Visible swelling in joints and limbs.
- Poor Appetite: A decrease in appetite and overall condition resulting in loss of weight.
- Infants may have delayed tooth eruption.

Treatment:
- Restart the squirrel on formula no matter what the age.
- Dietary Correction: Ensure a balanced diet rich in calcium and appropriate levels of phosphorus. Foods high in calcium include leafy greens (like kale and collard greens), broccoli, nuts, and beet greens. Rodent or squirrel blocks are balanced foods.
- Calcium Supplements: In severe cases, calcium supplements may be necessary under veterinary guidance.
- Vitamin D3 Supplementation: Providing adequate vitamin D3, either through diet, exposure to natural sunlight, or supplements.
- Exercise is important for bone development. Squirrels need lots of opportunities to climb and jump. (When ready of course)
- Supportive Care: Providing a safe and comfortable environment. They may appreciate a heating pad in one corner. Pain management.

Other Issues

Bloat

Bloat in baby squirrels is a serious condition that can occur due to several factors related to feeding and digestion.

- Feeding too much formula at one time can overwhelm the baby squirrel's digestive system.
- Using an inappropriate formula that is too rich or difficult to digest can lead to bloating. Cow milk is a good example.
- Feeding formula that is too cold can cause digestive issues. The formula should be warm (around body temperature).

Symptoms of Bloat:
- Swollen Abdomen: A noticeably enlarged and firm abdomen. A belly should look full but be soft feeling after a feeding.
- Discomfort and Restlessness: The baby squirrel may appear agitated or in pain.
- Lack of Appetite: Refusal to eat or reduced interest in feeding.
- Lethargy: Unusual tiredness or lack of activity.

Use a formula specifically designed for baby squirrels, such as Fox Valley and follow established frequency charts. Make sure to hold the baby in an upright position while feeding to prevent air swallowing. Ensure the formula is warmed to body temperature before feeding. Feed slowly and minimize them swallowing air.

To treat bloat give fluids such as a 50/50 Pedialyte water mix at the next feeding. You can give a couple drops of Simethicone, a human infant medication used in the management and treatment of flatulence. Gentle massage may help.

Remember to stimulate infants under five weeks to eliminate after each feeding.

Diarrhea

Healthy baby squirrels pee and poop several times a day after feeding and being stimulated. Normal feces should be firm and light-colored. If the stool appears loose, runny, or foul-smelling. This can occur if the baby is not properly transitioned to a new formula, is fed the wrong formula, or too frequently. Babies can be overfed, leading to an overstretched stomach.

To treat diarrhea, switch the baby back to an electrolyte hydration formula, such as Pedialyte or lactated Ringer's solution (with no more than 2.5% lactose), for a few feedings. Then, follow a proper schedule to transition the baby back onto the formula. If problems persist, the baby should be seen by a veterinarian.

Diarrhea can also be a symptom of internal parasites. So put the bowel movement under a scope and do a fecal exam or take a sample to your vet to check for parasite eggs.

Teeth Issues

Squirrel teeth start growing at three weeks and never stop! Consequently, they can have several dental problems. Part of the intake of a young squirrel is to carefully look in their mouth. If they do not have teeth yet check for healthy gums. If they have teeth count the teeth and make sure none are broken. Broken teeth can happen during a fall.

Malocclusion

Malocclusion is when the front incisors do not line up properly. They may have an overbite, or underbite, or the teeth grow at an odd angle. Because the squirrel's teeth grow constantly this can become a problem. The teeth may grow into the roof of the mouth or curve around the face.

The squirrel eventually may not be able to eat and starve to death.

Malocclusion may be caused by a fall, being hit by a car, or MBD. Some squirrels are just born with "bad teeth".

Learning to cut and trim squirrels' teeth is an important skill. Have your vet or an experienced squirrel rehabilitator teach you how to take care of the teeth safely.

An orange coloration is normal for squirrel teeth. The incisors start to turn orange at about four months of age.

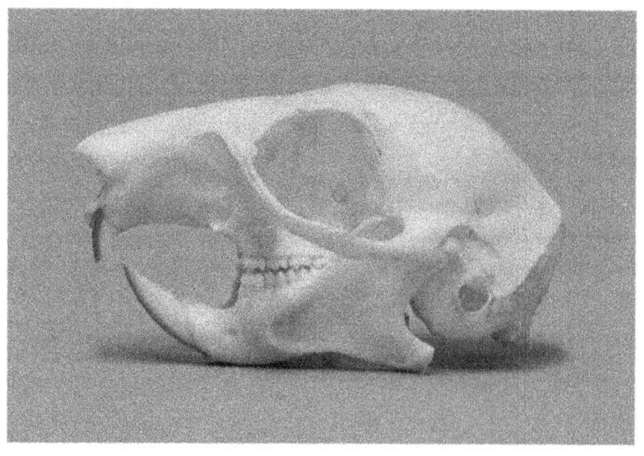

Normal red squirrel skull.
Photo:
Klaus Rassinger
Museum Wiesbaden

Cages & Enclosures

You will need several cages to handle squirrels as they grow and develop. I typically used 3 different sized enclosures during the first five months of life. At each stage of growth, I bump them up to a more suitable environment. For squirrels being released, they would be moved to an outdoor enclosure to prepare for freedom. I typically do a soft release with squirrels. A soft release means leaving them access to their outside enclosure and food sources while they become adjusted to living as wild animals.

Infants

Infant squirrels with eyes still closed just need a plastic tote or 10 gallon glass aquarium with wire lid. Incubators are fabulous. Place a heating pad in one half of the enclosure because the squirrel needs to be able to crawl off if they get to hot. Put a thermometer in with the baby to monitor the temperature but also place your hand in where the baby is sleeping to double check.

Eyes Open

Once they open there eyes they will start moving around and exploring. As there muscles gain strength and they start to thermoregulate they can be moved to a small wire cage. The distance between bars should be one half inch (.5 in or 1.2 cm). Cages made for hamsters and gerbils make good starter cages giving them more room to climb and develop muscles. Bird cages made for parakeets are also good. The height of bird cages can give them room to climb. These cages are still small enough to place on a counter or stand. Place the heating pad under the cage. This will keep the pad and its wiring away from growing teeth.

Explorers

As young squirrels start to try new foods they also begin to explore and play with each other. At this point, they are ready for a larger freestanding cage. I am a big fan of the Ferret Nation and Midwest Cages that are made for small mammals such as squirrels, and sugar gliders. Bird cages also make good enclosures.

Include places to sleep, hide, and play. Ferret-style hammocks are popular and wooden rabbit tunnels (especially for ground squirrels and chipmunks). My squirrels always loved bird toys. Get ones made for parrots because they are typically sturdy. Avoid anything with strings that can unravel and get tangled with their body.

Dishes

Don't use plastic dishes with squirrels because they will just eat them. Use ceramic dishes for food and then they are also easy to wash.

Water bottles

Squirrels are hell on water bottles.

Water bottles can be a problem. Even though they hang outside the cage the plastic ones will get chewed. Glass water bottles are better however more expensive. I have also had issues with them dripping. Squirrels will also figure out that they can stick a finger into the downspout and make water come out. They think this is great fun. Older squirrels can use a water dish although this can be messy! Use a shallow dish and change the water twice a day.

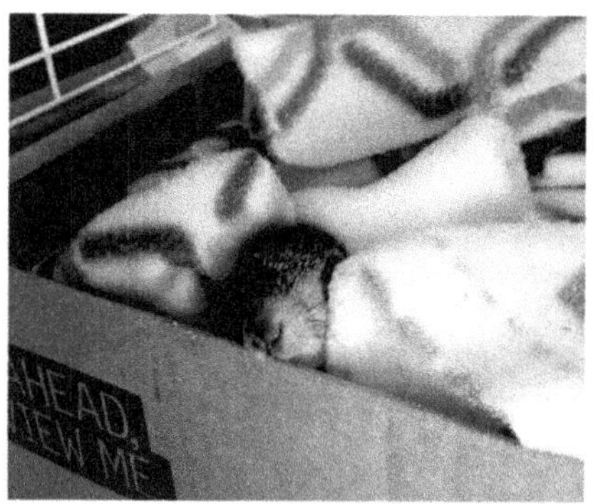

A cardboard box and some soft blankets can be a safe place to hide and take a nap.

Outdoor Enclosures

Squirrels born in the spring may be ready to go into an outdoor enclosure at 7 - 8 weeks of age. Some rehabilitators use the weight of 220 grams as a good marker. These babies are NOT weaned yet. However, they can be fed formula from outside the cage or even in a dish if there are just one or two babies (who aren't fighting over food). You need to remove formula dishes promptly so as not to attract flies. Red and gray squirrels should be housed separately and I will talk about that more in their species pages.

A soft release is when you still provide food and housing but leave access to the outdoors. My squirrels often spent a week making the transition to "freedom".

Ask for cage donations. People who have lost birds may not need their cage anymore. Someone gave me this fabulous one. Just remember to wash well so you don't bring in germs. Measure the space between bars to make sure it will accommodate a squirrel safely.

Outdoor homemade caging should be made of material such as hardware cloth or 1/2 by 1/2 welded wire. This will help prevent escape and also ensure the animal doesn't get stuck or injured in the wire. This also helps protect your squirrels from natural predators such as foxes. Bury the hardware cloth or wire approximately 12" below the surface, to prevent escape but also allow for natural digging opportunities. Branches for gnawing and climbing are important. Use native trees that are part of the squirrel's natural diet.

Tree squirrels require vertical height, and horizontal space for jumping. Flying squirrels need to be able to practice gliding. Platforms, rope, and wooden ladders such as those made for large birds provide climbing experiences. Include nest boxes for sleeping and hiding and have several so they don't fight over them.

An outside enclosure for tree squirrels should be a minimum of 8x8x8. So eight feet wide, eight feet long, and eight feet tall. (Miller). This would accommodate 2 - 3 squirrels. If you have 3 - 5 squirrels increase the size to 10x10x8 to accommodate movement and discourage aggression.

Not the best drawing but an example of an outdoor enclosure.

Cleaning Cages and Bedding

Keeping cages and bedding clean is very important and not always easy. When the environment is clean the animal is more likely to be healthy and happy. When babies are small that is easy. However, as they grow and we want to promote a natural fear to help them survive in the wild it can be hard to find ways to clean their enclosures without inducing stress.

Sunshine

Sunshine is a gift! It has many healing qualities both figuratively and literally. The sun's rays act as a natural disinfectant. I frequently hang bedding on the clothesline on a sunny day.
Getting animals out in the sun can help them grow, heal, and get some vitamin D. I often will put eyes open young babies outside in a wire cage in the yard (where I can monitor them). I use a cage that is wire on the bottom so they can feel and eat the grass. Groundhogs love this but so do squirrels. I cover half the cage with a blanket so they can choose shade and I typically have a box or log tunnel so they can hide if needed. Give them about an hour outside. This is also a great way to prepare them to make the transition to a grow-out cage. Monitor for safety!

Bleach

Sodium hypochlorite, commonly known as bleach is a good disinfectant. It is also not as harmful as some of the other chemicals used for cleaning (and its cheaper) 1 tablespoon of bleach per 1 quart of water is a good strength.
As I've said I love the Ferret Nation and Midwest Cages which come with trays that slide out. This makes it easy to clean. I take the tray out, dispose of manure and debris, wash the tray, rinse it with bleach solution and let it dry in the sun.

Flying squirrels need a cage that they can practice gliding in. A cage that is wide is good for this. This cage is the Borneo Version II from Exotic Nutrition.

Ground squirrels and chipmunks burrow. Give them opportunities to dig. You can bury some PVC drainage pipe in the ground to make a underground hiding space.

Don't Mix and Match!

Squirrels begin to get very territorial after they are weaned. Especially, red squirrels. Don't mix species after weaning and don't introduce a new member to an established juvenile group. Weaned juveniles and adults may be extremely aggressive and attack each other causing serious injury or death.

Tree squirrels will utilize nest boxes year round

Release Criteria and Considerations for Squirrels

1. **Health and Physical Condition**
   - Full Recovery: Ensure the squirrel has fully recovered from any injuries or illnesses.
   - Weight and Strength: The squirrel should be at a healthy weight and demonstrate sufficient strength and agility.
   - Fur Condition: The coat should be in good condition, free of mange, parasites, or significant fur loss.
2. **Behavioral Readiness**
   - Foraging Skills: The squirrel should be able to forage for food independently. Be able to eat an unshelled walnut.
   - Natural Behaviors: Display typical squirrel behaviors such as climbing, jumping, and nesting.
   - Fear of Humans: The squirrel should show a natural wariness of humans to ensure survival in the wild.
3. **Time of Year**
   - Seasonal Considerations: Ideally, release in spring (for fall born babies)or early fall (for spring born babies) when food is abundant, and weather conditions are mild.
   - Avoid Harsh Weather: Avoid releasing during extreme cold, heat, or during stormy weather.
   - Release in morning so they can survey the area and build a nest.
4. **Release Site Selection**
   - Suitable Habitat: Choose an area with plenty of trees and natural cover for shelter and nesting.
   - Food Availability: Ensure the area has a good supply of natural food sources, such as nuts, seeds, and berries.
   - Water Source: Proximity to a natural water source is beneficial for the squirrel's hydration needs.
   - Safety from Predators: Assess the site for predator presence and select areas with minimal human and pet interference.

5. **Gradual Acclimatization**
   - Soft Release: Consider a soft release, where the squirrel is gradually acclimated to the wild. This might involve providing a temporary release enclosure at the site.
   - Observation Period: Monitor the squirrel for a few days to ensure it is adapting well to the new environment.
6. **Post-Release Monitoring**
   - Regular Checks: Conduct regular checks to see if the squirrel is thriving. This could include direct observation or using motion-activated cameras.
   - Backup Plan: Have a plan in place to recapture the squirrel if it shows signs of distress or inability to survive.
7. **Legal and Ethical Considerations**
   - Permits and Regulations: Ensure that the release complies with local wildlife laws and regulations.
   - Public Awareness: Inform nearby residents (if in a suburban or urban area) about the release to minimize potential human-squirrel conflicts.
8. **Nest Box Provision**
   - Nest Box: Providing a nest box can offer initial shelter and protection, especially if natural nesting sites are limited.

Squirrels! Chipmunks!

Squirrels are fun, crazy, and so clever. Ever watch one strategize how to get in your bird feeder? They are determined and creative in their quest for food and shelter.

When you are doing any work in wildlife rehabilitation or conservation it is important to understand the life cycle, habitat, and behavior of the animal you are helping. In this section, we will go over individual squirrel and chipmunk species in order to help you understand and care for them better.

Squirrels are very widespread throughout the world. They are rodents and related to groundhogs and prairie dogs.
There are over 200 species worldwide inhabiting all continents except Antarctica and Oceania. North America has over 65 species of squirrels, including tree squirrels, ground squirrels, and flying squirrels.

Tree-dwellers include the American red squirrel (Tamiasciurus hudsonicus), Eastern gray (Sciurus carolinensis), Eastern Fox squirrels (Sciurus niger), and southern flying (Glaucomys volans). We also have a variety of ground squirrels and chipmunks such as the California ground squirrel (Otospermophilus beecheyi) and the Eastern Chipmunk (Tamias striatus).
Note all the different taxonomies and genera!! A very diverse group of animals.

In general, tree squirrels live independently and are very territorial. Flying squirrels and ground squirrels are more social and form a small group. Ground squirrels are territorial and live in loose colonies similar to prairie dogs.

Eastern/Western Gray Squirrel

The Eastern Gray Squirrel (Sciurus carolinensis) and the Western Gray Squirrel (Sciurus griseus) are two distinct species with several similarities and a few differences.

The eastern covers a broad range and is in all states east of the Mississippi River as well as into the Midwest. Introduced to many other parts of the world including the western United States, the United Kingdom, and parts of Europe where it is considered an invasive species and is displacing the native Eurasian red squirrel.

The Western Gray Squirrel prefers oak woodlands, coniferous forests, and riparian corridors and is less common in urban areas.
They are native to the western United States, specifically in California, Oregon, and Washington. Their range is more restricted compared to the Eastern Gray Squirrel.

East

West

Obviously, per their name gray squirrels are predominantly gray with a buff-colored belly. However, it's not uncommon for the eastern to have a brownish or reddish color. Western's have silvery-gray fur with a pure white or pale gray belly. The fur is generally more uniform in color than that of the Eastern Gray Squirrel.

In addition, especially in northern areas the melanistic (black color) has become more common. Scientists theorize this may be due to less predation and the black fur keeping animals warmer in colder climates.

Melanistic eastern gray squirrel
photo credit: D. Gordon E. Robertson

Their bodies are about fifteen to twenty inches in length including seven inches or so for the tail. They weigh around one to one and a half pounds. The Western Gray is slightly larger than the eastern. Gray squirrels are the most common squirrel species in the USA.

Generally solitary but can be seen in groups, especially during feeding. Eastern Gray Squirrels are more acclimated to urban areas.

Life Cycle

In general, gray squirrels often give birth twice a year in the early spring and late summer or early fall. Three to four kits are born in the litter.

The young are born naked and are blind and deaf and weigh only about 0.5 ounces or 14 grams. They can not produce body heat (thermoregulate) and are totally dependent on their mom. Fur begins to grow at one week and they open their eyes at about four weeks. They stay in the nest for the first six weeks of life.

They then start to explore with their mom supervising. This is a critical learning period where they develop essential skills such as climbing, foraging, and social interactions. At around 12 weeks, young squirrels become more independent but may still stay close to their natal area.

During adolescence (3-6 Months) juvenile squirrels continue to grow and develop. They practice building nests, storing food, and honing their survival skills. By the end of this period, they are fully independent and capable of surviving on their own.

The babies are called kits. Male squirrels are known as "boars" and female squirrels are called "sows". Males and females are similar as far as size and coloring. You often have to be able to see their sexual attributes to know if it's male or female.

Depending on the species tree squirrels build dens inside the hollow of a tree or nests called dreys. Dreys are built on the fork of a tree. Dens are typically in the hollow of a tree and lined with leaves and grasses.

Gray squirrels reach sexual maturity at around 10-12 months. At this stage, they are capable of reproducing and contributing to the next generation of squirrels. Squirrel courtship can be fun to observe. The males will chase the female with the dominant male often being the breeder. Squirrels do not form pair bonds and the male is not active in raising the offspring. Mother squirrels are very protective and will fight off predators trying to attack their babies.

As adults, gray squirrels lead solitary lives except during mating season or when mothers care for their young. They are active during the day (diurnal) and spend much of their time foraging for food.

In the wild, gray squirrels typically live for 6-12 years, though many do not survive their first year due to predation and other factors.

Caching

Gray squirrels are known for their behavior of caching, or storing, food for the winter. They bury nuts and seeds in various locations, a practice that not only helps them survive during lean months but also contributes to forest regeneration when forgotten caches sprout into new plants. They will also place food in tree cavities.

Gray squirrels are scatter hoarders. They spread food items across multiple locations. This method reduces the risk of losing the entire food supply to predators or competitors and ensures that some caches remain undiscovered. Squirrels typically dig small holes, deposit a single nut or seed, and then cover it with soil or leaves.

Gray squirrels are selective about the food they cache, often choosing nuts and seeds that are high in fat and protein and have a longer shelf life. Common choices include acorns, walnuts, and hazelnuts.

Before caching, squirrels may inspect and sometimes peel or clean the food item to ensure it is in good condition. This helps prevent mold and rot. Other animals, such as birds and other squirrels, may steal from caches. To mitigate this, gray squirrels often create false caches to deceive potential thieves.

Although not always visible to humans, squirrels use subtle markers or memory cues to remember the locations of their caches. They rely on spatial memory and the recognition of nearby landmarks. Gray squirrels have excellent spatial memory, which allows them to recall the locations of many of their caches. They also use their keen sense of smell to locate buried food, even under several inches of snow or soil.

Retrieval of caches is most crucial during the winter and early spring when fresh food is scarce. Squirrels spend considerable time digging up and consuming their stored food during these periods.

Not all cached food is retrieved, leading to the germination of seeds and the growth of new plants. This behavior significantly contributes to forest regeneration and the dispersal of various tree species. By caching and subsequently retrieving food, gray squirrels play a role in the distribution of resources within their ecosystems, influencing the availability of food for other animals.

Hibernation - Nope

Gray squirrels are crepuscular or more active during the early and late hours of the day and tend to avoid the heat in the middle of a summer day.

They do not hibernate, instead, they remain active throughout the year, although their activity levels and behaviors change with the seasons. They spend more time in their nests (dreys) to conserve energy and stay warm.

During particularly harsh weather, they may remain in their nests for several days at a time, venturing out only when necessary. Gray squirrels build and maintain warm, well-insulated nests to protect themselves from the cold. These nests are typically constructed high in trees and are made from twigs, leaves, moss, and other natural materials.

In addition to dreys, gray squirrels may also use tree cavities, abandoned bird nests, and human made nest boxes for shelter.

During winter, gray squirrels rely heavily on their cached food supplies. They dig up buried nuts and seeds to sustain themselves. They may also eat tree bark, fungi, and other available plant material when other food sources are scarce.

Gray squirrels have several physical adaptations that help them survive the winter. Their thick fur provides insulation against the cold, and their bushy tails can be wrapped around their bodies for extra warmth.

Predation

Gray squirrels, both Eastern (Sciurus carolinensis) and Western (Sciurus griseus), are common targets for a variety of predators due to their small size and abundance. Despite the numerous threats they face, Gray squirrels have developed several strategies to avoid predation and ensure their survival.

Common Predators of Gray Squirrels
- **Birds of Prey**
  - Hawks: Red-tailed hawks and Cooper's hawks are significant predators, using their keen eyesight and swift flight to catch squirrels.
  - Owls: Great horned owls and barred owls hunt squirrels, particularly at dawn, dusk, and nighttime when squirrels are less alert.
- **Mammalian Predators**
  - Foxes: Red foxes and gray foxes often prey on ground-foraging squirrels.
  - Coyotes: Opportunistic hunters that will catch squirrels if the opportunity arises.
  - Bobcats: Skilled climbers and hunters that can catch squirrels both on the ground and in trees.
  - Domestic Cats and Dogs: Pets can pose a threat, especially in urban and suburban areas.
- **Reptiles**
  - Snakes: Larger snakes, such as rat snakes, may prey on squirrels, particularly young ones or those in nests.
- **Humans**
   Hunting and Trapping: In some areas, humans hunt gray squirrels for sport or control measures.

Defense Mechanisms of Gray Squirrels

Gray squirrels are exceptionally agile and fast, capable of making quick, erratic movements to evade predators. Their ability to leap between branches and trees helps them escape many ground and aerial threats.

Gray squirrels have excellent vision and hearing, allowing them to detect approaching predators quickly. They are constantly vigilant, often pausing to scan their surroundings and listen for danger.

Squirrels use a variety of vocalizations and tail signals to alert other squirrels of nearby predators. These alarm calls can vary in tone and intensity depending on the type of threat.

Their gray fur provides some level of camouflage against tree bark and foliage. When threatened, squirrels may freeze and remain motionless to avoid detection.

They often have multiple escape routes planned in their territories. When pursued, they can quickly dart into nearby trees, bushes, or other cover.

Conservation Concerns

The eastern gray squirrel is common across its territory however the western gray squirrel is losing ground. This is in part due to the eastern gray entering its native range. Washington State has listed the western gray as endangered within its state. Primarily due to habitat loss and fragmentation, disease, road mortality, predation, and the impacts of climate change.

The Eastern Gray Squirrel Vs. the Eurasian Red Squirrel

You may have heard people in Great Britain or other parts of Europe say they were killing gray squirrels. Why?
The Eastern Gray Squirrel (Sciurus carolinensis) is native to North America but has been introduced to various parts of Europe, including the United Kingdom, Ireland, and Italy.

This introduction, by humans, has led to competition between the gray squirrel and the native Eurasian red squirrel (Sciurus vulgaris). Starting in the late 1800s through the 1950s, the Eastern Gray Squirrel was brought to Europe as pets and to also to be released as a sport-hunting animal (Wauters, 2023)

Gray squirrels are larger and more adaptable than red squirrels. They compete more effectively for food resources such as nuts, seeds, and berries. Gray squirrels often displace red squirrels from their habitats. Red squirrels are pushed into less optimal areas with fewer resources, which affects their population density and health.

One of the most significant problems is the transmission of squirrel pox virus. Gray squirrels carry the virus but suffer lower mortality, developing immunity (see this section under diseases).
When red squirrels contract the virus, it often leads to severe illness and high mortality rates. This has led to drastic declines in red squirrel populations in areas where the two species overlap.

Conservation efforts focus on protecting and restoring habitats that are favorable to red squirrels. This includes planting native coniferous trees and managing woodlands to support red squirrel populations.
Conservationists also work to control gray squirrel populations through culling and sterilization programs in areas where red squirrels are at risk.

Chipmunks

Chipmunks, with their distinctive stripes and cheek pouches, are some of the most endearing creatures in the animal kingdom. These small, agile rodents are a common sight in many parts of North America, scurrying across forest floors, gardens, and even urban parks.

There are 24 species native to the United States. The two most common species are the Eastern chipmunk and the Least chipmunk. Other species include the Allen's, Hopi, and Colorado.

Chipmunks are part of the larger squirrel family and are primarily found in North America. The genus Tamias is divided into three subgenera: Tamias (eastern chipmunks), Neotamias (western chipmunks), and Eutamias (Siberian chipmunks).

They are distinguished by their distinctive stripes and cheek pouches used for storing food. Their strips allow them to blend into the forest floor and making them harder for predators see. Their tails are long, straight, and furred but not fluffy like tree squirrels.

They look very similar however, chipmunks are smaller, on average 7.2 to 8.5 inches (18.5 to 21.6 centimeters). They have alternating light and dark stripes along their cheeks and down their backs.

They live in a variety of ecosystems including deserts, grasslands, and forests, and are numerous in urban parks. They live underground in burrows. However, they can and do climb trees.

The Hopi chipmunk
blends into its
desert environment.

Life Cycle of Chipmunks

Chipmunks typically mate twice a year, during the spring and late summer. Following a gestation period of about 31 days, the female gives birth to a litter of 2-6 young.

Chipmunk pups are born blind, hairless, and entirely dependent on their mother. They weigh just a few grams and are nurtured in a burrow, which provides protection from predators and harsh weather. By the eighth day of life, their stripes begin to appear.

At one month they have fur and their eyes are open.

After about six weeks, the pups begin to venture out of the burrow, though they continue to nurse until they are around two months old. During this period, they learn essential survival skills by observing their mother.

Eastern Chipmunk
Photo credit:
Gilles Gonthier

Juvenile Stage

Young chipmunks start exploring their surroundings, practicing foraging, and refining their motor skills. They remain close to the burrow, gradually expanding their range as they grow more confident. Independence: By the age of 2-3 months, juvenile chipmunks are ready to leave the maternal burrow and establish their own territories. This independence is crucial for reducing competition for resources among family members.

Adulthood

Chipmunks reach sexual maturity at about one year of age. As adults, they continue to forage, build burrows, and prepare for the breeding seasons.

Adult chipmunks are solitary and territorial. Each individual maintains its own burrow system, which can be quite extensive, including nesting chambers, food storage areas, and multiple entrances and exits.

In the wild, chipmunks typically live for 2-3 years, although some may live longer under optimal conditions.

Communication

Communication between eastern chipmunks is pretty interesting! It all starts with some chattering between the mother and her little ones. Chipmunks have five distinct vocalizations (de Silva et al. 2002). The loudest one is the chip, which they can repeat for up to thirty minutes. This chip is their way of saying, "Hey, I'm here!"

Then there's the chuck, a lower-pitched chip that shows anger, annoyance, or fear. Chucks are like warning signals, either indicating danger or serving as a threat among themselves. Trills are another vocalization they use for play or danger. These trills sound like screams and come into play when they're pouncing on each other or during mating and playing.

The chatter is a rapid growling sound you hear during confrontations, and it's also used between mothers and their babies. Chipmunks also have a whistle or scream, which they use in both happiness and fear.

Sometimes, you'll hear a whole chipmunk chorus when all the chipmunks in an area start singing together. This is called an "epideictic display," but no one really knows why they do it.

Besides their vocalizations, chipmunks mark their territory with urine and feces, and they have anal scent glands. The only other chemical communication they use is when females are in estrus.

Hibernation - Nope! Torpor - Yup

Instead of remaining in a deep sleep (hibernation) throughout the winter, chipmunks enter a state of torpor. During torpor, their body temperature drops, and their metabolism slows down significantly, allowing them to conserve energy.

Chipmunks periodically wake from their torpid state to eat from their food stores, which they gather and store in their burrows during the warmer months. This pattern of waking and sleeping continues throughout the winter. By waking up to eat, they ensure they have enough energy to survive until spring.

Cache

Unlike gray squirrels, chipmunks have a larder cache versus a scatter cache. Their main larder is in their burrow however they will have smaller ones nearby. During the warmer months, chipmunks are very active in collecting food. They gather seeds, nuts, berries, and other edible items from their surroundings.

Chipmunks have cheek pouches that they use to carry food back to their burrows. These pouches can expand significantly, allowing them to transport large amounts of food in one trip.

Once back at their burrows, chipmunks store the collected food in dedicated chambers. These storage chambers can be quite large and hold enough food to last through the winter.

Their burrows are intricate, with multiple chambers and tunnels. There are specific areas for sleeping, waste, and food storage. This organization helps them manage their food supply effectively. Burrows extend 12 –30 feet long and consist of a storage chamber, sleeping room (able to hold a half bushel), dump, and latrine with several entrances.

Habitat

Chipmunks live in a variety of habitats across North America. They thrive in deciduous and mixed forests, where they find abundant food sources and ample cover from predators.

They often build their burrows near trees, fallen logs, or rock piles, which provide additional protection and support for their intricate tunnel systems.

Chipmunks also inhabit shrublands and brushy areas, where dense vegetation offers excellent cover and foraging opportunities. These areas provide a variety of berries, seeds, and insects.

Chipmunks are highly adaptable and can thrive in urban and suburban environments. Gardens, parks, and yards offer plentiful food and nesting sites. They often come into contact with humans. While they can sometimes be considered pests due to their burrowing habits, they also play a role in controlling insect populations and dispersing seeds.

Some chipmunk species prefer rocky habitats, where they use natural crevices and gaps between rocks to build their nests. These environments offer protection from predators and harsh weather conditions.

The Least Chipmunk: A Small Wonder of the Rodent World
The least chipmunk (Neotamias minimus) is a captivating and diminutive member of the chipmunk family. Known for its agility and distinctive appearance, the least chipmunk is a common sight in North America's boreal forests, alpine regions, and scrublands.

They are about about 7-9 inches in total length, including its tail, and typically weigh between 1 and 2 ounces.

Despite its small size, this tiny rodent plays a significant role in its ecosystem. By caching and sometimes forgetting about their food stores, least chipmunks play a crucial role in seed dispersal and forest regeneration.

Least Chipmunk

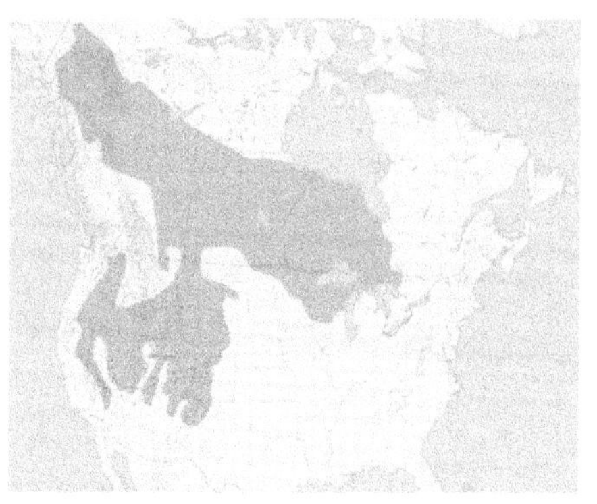

Least chipmunk is common in higher elevations and boreal/Tiago forests

Fox Squirrels

Fox Squirrels (Sciurus niger) are one of the most fascinating and adaptable species in North America. Known for their vibrant reddish-brown fur and bushy tails, these squirrels play a significant role in their ecosystems.

Fox Squirrels are larger than grays and range from eighteen to twenty-seven inches and up to two and a half pounds (2.5). They have salt and pepper gray hair on their backs with yellow to orange coloring on their upper body parts. With pale yellow to bright orange bellies. Tails have yellow tips.

Fox Squirrels and grays occupy much of the same habitat. Fox squirrels prefer a more wooded area and are not as likely in heavily urban areas with fewer trees where as grays have better adapted to urban areas. They prefer older growth without dense undergrowth.

In urban environments, Fox Squirrels often inhabit parks, gardens, and neighborhoods with mature trees.

Fox Squirrels prefer open woodlands with a mix of tree species, especially those that produce nuts, such as oaks and hickories. These trees provide both food and nesting sites. They are also proficient at utilizing cavities in trees, either natural or those created by woodpeckers, for nesting and shelter. They are diurnal, meaning they are most active during the day, particularly in the early morning and late afternoon.

Range of the Fox Squirrel

Life Cycle

Fox squirrels follow a life cycle that begins with a brief mating season, usually in late winter and early summer. Females give birth to two litters per year, with the gestation period lasting about 44 days. The typical litter size ranges from two to four kits.

The kittens are born blind and hairless, relying entirely on their mother for warmth and nourishment. Their eyes open at about four to five weeks, and they begin to venture out of the nest at around seven to eight weeks old. By ten weeks, the young squirrels are weaned and start learning to forage and climb, although they may stay close to their mother for a few more weeks.

Fox squirrels reach sexual maturity at around ten to twelve months. In the wild, their lifespan averages six to seven years, though they can live longer in captivity.

Infant fox squirrel
Photo credit: Travis Witt

Fox Squirrels also have geographical color morphs. This Sherman Fox Squirrel black morph (S. n. shermani) is from central Florida.

Vocalization

Fox Squirrels are known for their diverse and interesting vocalizations, which they use to communicate with each other in various contexts.

Types of Vocalizations

Chattering and Clucking:

Fox squirrels often produce a series of sharp, repetitive sounds that can be described as chattering or clucking. These sounds are typically used as alarm calls to alert other squirrels of potential danger, such as predators or human presence.

Quaa:

This is a prolonged, more nasal-sounding alarm call compared to the chattering. It serves a similar purpose of alerting other squirrels to threats but is generally used in situations perceived as more urgent.

Moan:

A softer, drawn-out sound is often heard during more relaxed interactions. This can be a form of communication between mothers and their young or between individuals in close proximity. Rehabilitators often hear this sound from young fox squirrels.

Muk-Muk:

A quiet, repetitive call used primarily by males during mating season to communicate with females. This sound is non-aggressive and is intended to attract a mate or signal presence.

Apart from vocalizations, fox squirrels also use body language and scent marking to communicate. Tail flicking is a common visual signal that accompanies vocal alarms, adding emphasis to the warning. Scent marking through glands located on their cheeks and paws helps establish territories and convey information about individual identity and reproductive status.

Diet of the Fox Squirrel

Fox squirrels have a varied and adaptable diet that changes with the seasons and the availability of food sources. Their diet includes a mix of plant material, nuts, seeds, fruits, fungi, and occasionally animal matter.

1. **Spring and Summer:**
   - During the warmer months, fox squirrels consume a variety of green vegetation, including buds, flowers, and young leaves.
   - They also eat a range of fruits and berries, which provide essential vitamins and moisture.
   - Insects and small invertebrates may be consumed as an additional protein source.
2. **Autumn:**
   - Fall is a critical time for fox squirrels as they prepare for winter. They focus on gathering and consuming high-energy foods such as acorns, hickory nuts, walnuts, and other seeds.
   - Agricultural crops such as corn, various beans, oats, wheat, and apples are also consumed.
   - This is the peak time for caching, where they store surplus food for the winter months.
3. **Winter:**
   - In winter, their diet relies heavily on cached food. They dig up their stored nuts and seeds, which provide the necessary calories to sustain them through the cold months.
   - They may also eat bark, fungi, and lichen when other food sources are scarce.

Caching

Caching, or the storing of food for later use, is a crucial survival strategy for fox squirrels. This behavior ensures they have a reliable food source during the winter when fresh food is scarce.

Fox squirrels practice scatter hoarding, where they bury individual nuts or seeds in separate locations rather than in a single stash. This method reduces the risk of losing all their food to predators or competitors.

They rely on spatial memory to relocate their caches. Studies have shown that fox squirrels use both memory and scent to find their stored food, even months after caching it.

Fox squirrels are known to periodically check and move their caches. This behavior, called "recaching," helps protect their food from being discovered by other animals and ensures that their storage remains effective.

Mikel M. Delgado who studies squirrel behavior has found that the eastern fox squirrel will organize their caches according to the variety of nuts and seeds. In a study of 45 fox squirrels, he found that they would organize there nuts and remember which type of nut was buried at which location. He states that this behavior demonstrated " spatial chunking in a scatter hoarder underscores the cognitive demand of scatter-hoarding" (Delgado).

Like other squirrel species, fox squirrels play a significant role in forest ecology through their caching behavior. By burying nuts and seeds, they inadvertently aid in seed dispersal and the regeneration of trees and plants. This contributes to forest health and biodiversity.

Ground Squirrel

Ground squirrels are a diverse group of small mammals belonging to the family Sciuridae. (23 species and 119 subspecies). Known for their burrowing habits and distinctive behaviors, they play a significant role in their ecosystems. These squirrels are distinct from tree squirrels because they nest in burrows, spending much of their time on the ground rather than in trees.

They have adapted to a variety of habitats from grasslands to forests. They have developed keen senses and quick reflexes to avoid predators and thrive in diverse environments.

Within Sciuridae, the subfamily Xerinae includes ground squirrels, chipmunks, prairie dogs, and marmots. I will not be talking about marmots or prairie dogs in this book but I wanted to let you know how broad this family is.

- Ground squirrels are spread across several genera, with Spermophilus (European and Asian species) being numerous. Other genera include Urocitellus, Ictidomys, and Otospermophilus.

- Otospermophilus. includes ground squirrels and what we often refer to as rock squirrels and are common in the southwest and western coastal states.
- Ictidomys includes the thirteen-lined ground squirrel (Ictidomys tridecemlineatus) found in grasslands throughout the US Great Plains and midwest states as well as Canada.
- Urocitellus is a group of ground squirrels that live in the northern and western parts of North America through the north-western United States and western Canada.

Ground squirrels are known for their complex social structures, especially in species like the California ground squirrel (Otospermophilus beecheyi). These animals exhibit a range of vocalizations and behaviors to communicate and protect their colonies from predators.

Life Cycle

The life cycle of ground squirrels begins with a mating season that typically occurs in early spring. After a gestation period of about 25 to 30 days, females give birth to a litter of pups, usually ranging from four to eight offspring.

Like other squirrels, newborns are altricial, meaning they are born blind, hairless, and completely dependent on their mother for warmth and nutrition. They develop rapidly, opening their eyes at around three weeks of age and starting to explore outside the burrow at about five to six weeks old.

The pups make short trips outside the burrow entrance, staying close to the safety of their home. They learn to forage for food, interact with siblings, and become more aware of their surroundings.

Around the same time they start exploring outside, the young are weaned off their mother's milk. They transition to a diet of solid food, which includes seeds, nuts, and vegetation.

Juvenile ground squirrels spend the summer learning to forage and avoid predators. By the time they are about three months old, ground squirrels are usually fully independent. They may continue to live near their natal burrow but establish their own territories and burrows as they mature.

By the time they reach about one year old, they are sexually mature and ready to reproduce.

Ground squirrels have a relatively short lifespan, averaging around three to five years in the wild, though some individuals may live longer under favorable conditions.

The Thirteen Lined Ground Squirrel lives in prairie habitat

The Arctic Ground Squirrel lives in the tundra of Northern Canada and Alaska.

The California Ground Squirrel lives in the western coastal states and parts of Nevada.

Ground squirrels give birth in burrows, which they dig themselves or inherit from previous generations. These burrows are complex tunnel systems that provide protection from predators and harsh weather conditions. They have nesting chambers, designated areas within the burrow system where the female ground squirrel prepares a nest for giving birth. The nest is typically lined with soft materials such as grasses, leaves, and fur to provide warmth and comfort for the newborns.

Burrows often have several entrances and exits, which help the squirrels escape predators and improve ventilation within the burrow system. Some burrows have separate chambers for storing food, which the mother squirrel uses to sustain herself during the early nursing period.

Diet

Ground squirrels have a varied diet that reflects their omnivorous nature. Their diet primarily consists of:

1. Plants: They consume a wide range of vegetation, including grasses, leaves, stems, and seeds. During spring and summer, fresh green vegetation forms a significant part of their diet.
2. Nuts and Seeds: Ground squirrels are adept at finding and storing nuts and seeds, which provide essential nutrients and energy. Acorns, sunflower seeds, and other available seeds are common dietary staples.
3. Fruits and Berries: When in season, fruits and berries become an important food source, providing vitamins and hydration.
4. Insects and Small Animals: Ground squirrels also eat insects, small vertebrates, and carrion, especially when plant-based food is scarce. This protein-rich diet helps them meet their nutritional needs.
5. Human Food: In areas where humans are present, ground squirrels may scavenge and consume discarded food, bird seed, and crops, sometimes causing conflicts with humans.

Habitat

Ground squirrels inhabit a variety of environments, from grasslands and savannas to forests and arid deserts. They are highly adaptable and can thrive in regions with different climatic conditions.

1. Burrows: Ground squirrels are expert burrowers, creating extensive underground tunnel systems. These burrows serve as shelters, nurseries, and storage areas for food. Burrow systems can be quite complex, with multiple entrances and chambers.
2. Open Areas: They prefer open habitats where they can watch for predators and quickly retreat to their burrows. Grasslands, meadows, and prairies are ideal environments.
3. Edge Habitats: Ground squirrels often thrive in edge habitats where forests meet open areas, benefiting from the diversity of food resources and cover.
4. Human-Altered Landscapes: They are also found in agricultural fields, parks, and suburban areas, where they take advantage of the abundant food resources.

Conservation

While many ground squirrel species are abundant, some face threats from habitat loss, agricultural practices, and human-wildlife conflicts. Conservation efforts focus on habitat preservation and mitigating human-wildlife interactions. Educating the public about coexistence strategies and the ecological benefits of ground squirrels is also essential. The Mohave ground squirrel is listed as threatened in California and the Northern Idaho ground squirrel is federally listed as threated.

Northern/Southern Flying Squirrel

Flying squirrels are fascinating creatures that captivate our imagination with their unique ability to glide through the forest canopy. Unlike their name suggests, they don't actually fly but use a special membrane to glide between trees.

The flying squirrel is a tree dweller but it has a unique method of transportation. The flying squirrel has large flaps of skin called patagia which gives them a square shape when they extend their limbs. Their tail provides stability.

This adaptation helps them escape predators, forage for food, and move efficiently through their arboreal habitat.

Flying squirrels belong to the family Sciuridae and are found across North America, Europe, and Asia. There are about 50 species of flying squirrels, with the most well-known being the Northern flying squirrel (Glaucomys sabrinus) and the Southern flying squirrel (Glaucomys volans) in North America.

Southern

Glaucomys volans

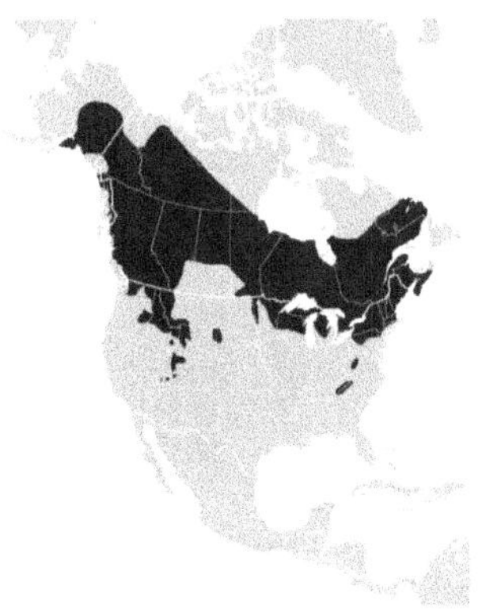

Northern

Glaucomys sabrinus

Northern versus Southern

Northern Flying Squirrel (Glaucomys sabrinus):
- Distribution: Found in the coniferous and mixed forests of North America, primarily in Canada, Alaska, the Pacific Northwest, and parts of the northern United States.
- Size: Slightly larger than their southern counterparts, with a body length of 10-13 inches, including the tail.
- Coloration: Typically have a gray-brown or reddish-brown coat with a lighter, creamy belly.
- Prefer coniferous and mixed forests, particularly those with a high density of old-growth trees and abundant fungal food sources. They thrive in cooler, more northern climates.

Southern Flying Squirrel (Glaucomys volans):
- Distribution: Found in the eastern United States and parts of Central America, inhabiting deciduous and mixed forests.
- Size: Smaller than the northern species, with a body length of 8-10 inches, including the tail.
- Coloration: Generally have a more grayish coat with a white belly, which helps distinguish them from the northern species.
- Favor deciduous and mixed forests with a variety of hardwood trees. They are more adaptable to different forest types and are often found in suburban and urban areas with sufficient tree cover.

Northern

*****Flying Squirrels ARE NOT Sugar Gliders!**
Sugar Gliders (Petaurus breviceps) are marsupials native to Australia. They are closely related to the possum with very different nutritional needs than flying squirrels. **Never feed flying squirrels commercial diets that are made for sugar gliders.**

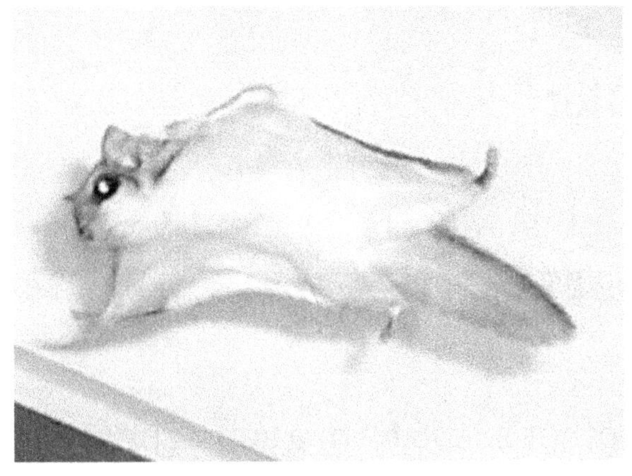

The flying squirrel does not actually fly. It glides. This mobility pattern is also seen in bats and flying lizards as well as the extinct pterosaurs

Photo by Michael Hays

Life Cycle

Flying squirrels typically mate once or twice a year, with mating seasons varying by species and region. For example, Northern flying squirrels often mate in late winter and early spring, while Southern flying squirrels can have two breeding seasons: one in early spring and another in late summer.

After a gestation period of about 40 days, the female gives birth to a litter of 2-6 young in a secure nest.

Newborn flying squirrels are born blind, hairless, and completely dependent on their mother. They develop quickly, with their eyes opening at about four weeks and fur fully developing by five weeks.

At around two months old, the young begin to practice gliding and foraging independently, though they may remain with their mother for a bit longer for protection and learning.

Flying squirrels reach sexual maturity at about one year of age. In the wild, they can live up to six years, though many do not survive that long due to predation and other environmental factors.

Diet

Flying squirrels have a diverse diet that reflects their omnivorous nature. Their food preferences include:

1. Nuts and Seeds:
   - Acorns, hickory nuts, and other seeds form a substantial part of their diet, especially in the fall when they prepare for winter.
2. Fruits and Berries:
   - They consume a variety of fruits and berries, which provide essential nutrients and hydration.
3. Fungi and Lichens:
   - Flying squirrels have a unique ability to digest fungi, including mycorrhizal fungi, which they find on tree trunks and in the soil. This plays a crucial role in forest ecology by aiding in the spread of fungal spores.
4. Insects and Bird Eggs:
   - They also eat insects, bird eggs, and small invertebrates, providing a protein boost to their diet.
5. Tree Sap and Bark:
   - Occasionally, they feed on tree sap and bark, especially during times when other food sources are scarce.

Southern

Habitat

Flying squirrels are highly adaptable and can thrive in various forested environments. Key aspects of their habitat include:

Forested Areas:

They are primarily found in deciduous and mixed forests, where they have ample trees for gliding and nesting. Old-growth forests are particularly important as they provide the necessary cavities for nesting.

Nesting Sites:

Flying squirrels use tree cavities, often created by woodpeckers or natural decay, for nesting. They may also use abandoned nests of other animals or construct their own leaf nests (dreys) in the branches of trees.

Nocturnal Lifestyle:

As nocturnal creatures, they are most active at night, which helps them avoid many predators and reduces competition for food with diurnal species.

Seasonal Movements:

In colder climates, flying squirrels may use communal nesting sites to conserve warmth during winter. They do not hibernate but may reduce their activity during extreme cold.

They live in nests or tree holes and can glide up to one hundred and fifty feet. They are nocturnal and not observed as often as other species. Flying squirrels eat a more varied diet and are omnivores.

American Red Squirrels

American red squirrels (Tamiasciurus hudsonicus) are lively and vocal inhabitants of North American forests. Recognizable by their reddish fur and white underbellies. They are native to North America, found predominantly in the coniferous forests of Canada, Alaska, and the northern United States.

They belong to the family Sciuridae, which includes other tree squirrels, ground squirrels, and flying squirrels. These squirrels are known for their territorial behavior and loud, chattering calls, which they use to communicate and defend their territory.

They are one of three species in the genus Tamiasciurus. The other two are the Douglas squirrel, T. douglasii, and the southwestern red squirrel, T. fremonti.

American red squirrels are relatively small. The total length, including the tail, is about 11.8 to 15 inches (30 to 38 cm). They typically weigh between 7 to 10 ounces (200 to 280 grams). Red squirrels have (you guessed it) reddish fur with a white underbelly.

Red squirrels, being smaller and more agile, are more territorial and aggressive in defending their smaller territories and food caches.

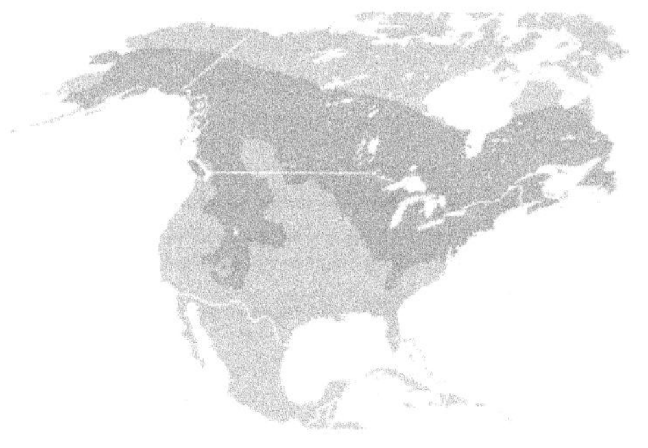

Approximate range of the
American Red Squirrel.
Image by Izvora

In the section on the Eastern Gray Squirrel, I wrote about how they have become an invasive species in Europe and displaced the Eurasian red squirrel. This is also becoming an issue in North America. While American Red Squirrels and Eastern Gray Squirrels do coexist in some regions, competition for resources and habitat can lead to the displacement of red squirrels in areas where gray squirrels are more abundant.

Conservation efforts focused on habitat management and preservation are essential to support the coexistence and health of both species.

Gray squirrels are more generalist feeders and can exploit a wider range of food sources, which gives them a competitive edge in diverse habitats. American red squirrels are highly territorial and defend their territories aggressively against intruders, including gray squirrels. This territorial behavior helps red squirrels maintain access to food resources and nesting sites within their territory.

In regions where gray squirrels are more abundant, they can outcompete red squirrels for food and nesting sites, potentially leading to a decline in red squirrel populations.

Human activities that fragment habitats can exacerbate competition. Red squirrels may be pushed into smaller, less optimal areas, while gray squirrels are better able to exploit fragmented and urbanized environments.

Managing forests to support a mix of coniferous and deciduous trees can help maintain suitable habitats for both species.
Conservation efforts that focus on preserving large tracts of continuous forest can benefit red squirrels by reducing habitat fragmentation.

Life Cycle

1. **Mating and Reproduction:**
   - American red squirrels have a breeding season that typically occurs twice a year, in late winter and mid-summer.
   - After a gestation period of about 31-35 days, females give birth to a litter of 3-7 young in a nest, called a drey, which is made from twigs, leaves, and moss.
2. **Development:**
   - The young are born blind, hairless, and dependent on their mother for warmth and nourishment. Their eyes open around 3-4 weeks of age, and they begin to grow fur shortly thereafter.
   - By 7-8 weeks old, the young start to explore outside the nest and learn to forage and climb.
3. **Maturity:**
   - Juvenile squirrels become independent at around 12 weeks old and reach sexual maturity by 9-10 months.
   - In the wild, American red squirrels typically live 2-5 years, although they can live longer in favorable conditions.

Diet

American red squirrels have a diverse diet that changes with the seasons:

1. **Conifer Seeds:**
   - They are particularly fond of conifer seeds, especially those from pine, spruce, and fir trees. They often harvest and store these seeds in caches, or middens, to ensure a food supply through the winter.
2. **Nuts and Seeds:**
   - In addition to conifer seeds, they eat acorns, hazelnuts, and other seeds they can find in their habitat.
3. **Fungi:**
   - Red squirrels consume various fungi, which they also store in caches for winter consumption.
4. **Fruits and Berries:**
   - They eat fruits and berries when available, which provide essential vitamins and hydration.
5. **Bark and Tree Sap:**
   - In winter, when other food sources are scarce, they may strip bark to access the underlying cambium layer and drink tree sap.
6. **Insects and Bird Eggs:**
   - Occasionally, they eat insects, bird eggs, and small invertebrates to supplement their diet.

Habitat

American red squirrels are most commonly found in coniferous and mixed forests:

Coniferous Forests:

These forests provide an abundance of conifer seeds, their primary food source. They thrive in boreal forests, which are rich in pine, spruce, and fir trees.
Mixed Woodlands:

They also inhabit mixed forests with a combination of coniferous and deciduous trees

.

Nesting Sites:

Red squirrels build nests, or dreys, in tree branches or use tree cavities for shelter. They often have multiple nests within their territory for sleeping and raising their young.

Territorial Behavior:

American red squirrels are highly territorial. They defend their territories aggressively, marking them with scent glands and vocalizing loudly to ward off intruders.

Conservation
While American red squirrels are not currently endangered, they face threats from habitat loss and competition with larger squirrel species, such as the eastern grey squirrel. Conservation efforts focus on preserving their natural habitats and managing forest ecosystems to support their populations.

Ways To Keep In The Know!

YouTube @foxruneec

Website: www.foxruneec.org

Patreon - patreon.com/foxruneec

PLEASE leave a written review for Amazon using this QR code or one wherever you purchased this book. It helps me out a great deal and lets me know what you liked or think I should do better next time. I appreciate you!

Thank You
for your support!
Ame

Biography

Ame Vanorio is an organic farmer, environmental educator, and wildlife rehabilitator. She was raised on a traditional Kentucky farm with horses, cattle, and tobacco. When not pulling weeds she was sneaking off to the back fields to sit quietly communing with wildlife. She rescued numerous baby rabbits, squirrels, and birds that were orphaned or injured due to farm activities like tree work & mowing.

Ame's hands-on experience includes:
- 30 years in education
- 17 years working in wildlife conservation and rehabilitation. I worked for Nation Wildlife Federation during college and for 12 years had my own center.
- Volunteering with Audubon, Sierra, club as well as my own Fox Run EEC to monitor wildlife and teach free environmental education to minimalized populations.

She holds graduate degrees in Education and Environmental Science and is the Founder/Director of Fox Run Environmental Education Center. Fox Run EEC is a non-profit that teaches organic agriculture, nature education, and wildlife conservation.

Check Out My Amazon Author Page - Take a pic of the QR Code below

Resources

Where to purchase supply's

Amazon

Amazon offers a great selection of pet supplies and can be a good source for hard to find things. I get my enclosures through them. Please go to my website and follow any Amazon link to their page. I may receive a small (1-3%) commission on purchases which helps us out in supporting new wildlife rehabilitators. If you are a licensed wildlife rehabilitator Amazon is great for making a wish list and sharing it with your followers.

Henry's Pets

Online pet store that specializes in products geared toward raising small pets.   They carry a line of rehabilitation supplies such as heating pads, formula, supplements, and pest treatments. Discounts for licensed wildlife rehabilitators. I've ordered from them several times and had excellent service.
www.henryspets.com

Exotic Nutrition

Online pet store for exotic pets. They have some good enclosure options, toys and climbing apparatus, and a nice nesting box. They also carry a brand of squirrel food but avoid the treat foods.
https://exoticnutrition.com/

Locally

Many things on my medical cabinet checklist (Free Download on my website) are things you can get locally either at a big box store, feedstore, or your local family pharmacy. In fact I encourage you to develop local relationships as they can be great about giving donations to local charities. If you do not have a garden a great way to get fresh produce for your animals is at a local farmers market.

Resources cont.

International Wildlife Rehabilitation Council

They offer a monthly free webinar (Coffee and Tea) and several high-quality courses. Also their course "The Basics" is required by many states for licensing. Courses have In-Person and Online options. If courses are beyond your budget email them and ask if any scholarship monies are available. Sometimes they have assistance. Membership includes their journal and course discounts.
https://theiwrc.org/

America Veterinary Medical Association (AVMA)

Great website with lots of resources however some information is behind an expensive membership pay wall.
 https://www.avma.org/

Cornell Wildlife Health Lab

Lots of information and resources on their website.
https://cwhl.vet.cornell.edu/

Merck Veterinary Manual

Being older I still use the print manual! However the website has a lot of high quality articles with images. This is made for domestic animals but much of the information is transferable and they are increasingly referencing exotic pets.
https://www.merckvetmanual.com/

References
Articles and Research Papers

Casey, S., & Goldthwait, M. (2012). **Etiologies and treatments of genital injuries of juvenile squirrels in rehabilitation.** Wildlife Rehabilitation Resources: Squirrels, 101-109.
https://www.ewildagain.org/squirrel-genital-injuries

Casey, S. & Casey, A. (2009)
Tips to Prevent Aspiration in Juvenile Squirrels
https://www.ewildagain.org/feeding-nipple-for-rehab-squirrels

Delgado, Mikel (2014) **Fox Squirrels Match Food Assessment and Cache Effort to Value and Scarcity.**
https://journals.plos.org/plosone/articleid=10.1371/journal.pone.0092892

Fericean, L. M., Banatean-Dunea, I., Ostan, M., Prunar, S., Prunar, F., Stef, R., & Rada, O. **(2022). Observation on the feeding behavior of orphaned baby red squirrels Sciurus vulgaris raised in captivity between 3 and 12 weeks.**

Grant, Kerrin. (2009). **Nutrition of Tree-dwelling Squirrels.** The veterinary clinics of North America. Exotic animal practice. 12. 287-97, ix. 10.1016/j.cvex.2009.01.015.

Hardee, C. (ND)
Rehabilitation of Eastern Gray Squirrels and Southern Flying Squirrels
Wildlife Rehabilitation Center of Central Florida PDF
www.wildlifecenterflorida.org

Linzey, D. W., & Linzey, A. V. (1979). **Growth and Development of the Southern Flying Squirrel (Glaucomys volans volans)**. Journal of Mammalogy, 60(3), 615–620. https://doi.org/10.2307/1380104 (This is an older article but has some good pictures of baby flyers with information on their age)

Miller, Erica, DVM. (2012) **MINIMUM STANDARDS FOR WILDLIFE REHABILITATION** Fourth Edition
Available from IWRC and online as a PDF

da Silva, Karen & Mahan, Carolyn & Silva, Jack. (2002). **The trill of the chase: Eastern chipmunks call to warn kin.** Journal of Mammalogy. 83. 546-552. 10.1644/1545-1542(2002)083<0546:TTOTCE>2.0.CO;2.

Wauters Lucas A. & Lurz Peter W. W. et.al. (2023) **Interactions between native and invasive species: A systematic review of the red squirrel-gray squirrel paradigm** Frontiers in Ecology and Evolution V.11, 2023.
https://www.frontiersin.org/journals/ecology-and-evolution/articles/10.3389/fevo.2023.1083008

www.ingramcontent.com/pod-product-compliance
Lightning Source LLC
Chambersburg PA
CBHW081220260726
48653CB00010BB/3713